Journey of Hope

Memoirs of a Mexican Girl

Rosalina Rosay

AR Publishing Company
Los Angeles, California
www.arpublish.com

www.HopeInMexico.com

Orders, inquiries, and contact info:

www.arpublish.com

ISBN-13: 978-0-9800361-7-6
ISBN-10: 0-9800361-7-8

Library of Congress Control Number: 2007908073
Library of Congress subject headings:
Rosay, Rosalina
Mexican American women – California – Los Angeles –
 Biography
Mexican American women – Biography
Immigrants – California – Biography
Immigrants – Mexico – Biography
Mexican American college students
Women authors, Mexican American
California – Biography
Illegal Immigrants
Amnesty – United States

Printed in the United States of America

To my children, Alex, Andrew, and Ariana,
who after reading this book, love and appreciate
America even more

~ ~ ~

And to my brothers, Jose and Alfonso, who have
shown great kindness throughout the years

Contents

Acknowledgments..................................5

Author's Notes.......................................6

Part One: Poverty and Deprivation......9

Part Two: Hope and Opportunity.....119

Epilogue...168

Final Thoughts...................................169

Acknowledgments

Thank you to my wonderful caring husband, Claude, who with his publishing experience, helped make this book a reality.

To Victor Wortman for his support throughout this experience and for his help editing the initial and final versions.

To Bob Cody for his attention to detail in editing my work.

Author's Notes

Some of the names in this book have been changed in order to maintain the privacy of certain individuals.

Most of the book was written to reflect the vocabulary and wisdom of the child and teen at that particular time.

About the Cover

The picture on the front cover is the street where I grew up. The appearance of the street has not changed much (the cobblestones have been paved over). What has changed is the number of people out on the street. In the late sixties and early seventies at six o'clock in the evening – the time of day when the picture was taken – you would see kids playing, moms gossiping, and people running errands. This was the time when moms were finished cleaning up after the three o'clock supper, dads were done with their siestas, and kids were finished with their homework.

The street is now empty because most of the houses have either been abandoned or the parents who stayed behind have passed away. Most of the people who used to live here now live in America.

The picture on the back cover is the plaza, and it is also a recent picture. The plaza has not changed much since I lived there. Like my street, the plaza seems empty.

Part One

Poverty and Deprivation

I do not know exactly how old I was when I started to admire America, but I think I was quite young because my memory of this feeling is more foggy and distant than any other. Even at that young age, I knew that America was a place where dreams could come true and once you made it there, you would never want to leave.

I guess I knew this because my oldest sister, Teresa, (who was old enough to be my mother) was already working in America – or El Norte (The North) as we usually called it. She headed there after her husband left her and their three kids. She was working as a maid and nanny and would always send money for her children.

Her kids lived in our house and she actually sent more than money. She sent beautiful clothes, made from all kinds of soft wonderful materials – unlike our regular clothes which, for the girls, consisted of stiff cotton dresses made by our neighbor. She also sent white, creamy, fragrant soaps that were easy to hold and much different than the big, brown, non-fragrant bars of soap the whole family normally shared. But what I loved the most were the pictures she sent – bright, colorful pictures of her and the children she cared for. These pictures showed their beautiful pool, with water that looked so clean and blue that I could not believe my eyes. The pictures also showed lush green gardens and the inside of the family's house, which to me was even nicer than the houses shown on Mexican soap operas.

My two oldest brothers, Jose and Alfonso, (who were also old enough to be my parents) were living in

America as well. They were working as gardeners and whenever my oldest brother, Jose, was deported back to Mexico, he would immediately try to get back to the United States. He hated returning to our house – a crowded mud-brick house with dirt floors and no bathroom.

Unlike America, Mexico around the late sixties was a very bad place to live, especially for children. There were so many of us. My mother had six sons and four daughters – not including the ones that had died as babies. Most women my mother's age had eight, nine, ten kids, often giving birth to babies around the same time as did their oldest daughters as was the case in our family.

With so many children in our town, it was very difficult for most kids to obtain the love, respect, and attention that they needed. If you had parents that lived in America sending you money, you got respect. If you were pretty, you got love. If you were a male, you got attention. I had none of the things that seemed to make a kid special.

Just like our town, our house at this time was full of kids – six of my mom's own kids, my oldest sister's three kids (whom I called my cousins because the girls were older than me and the boy was only a year younger) and two babies on the way. One of the babies on the way belonged to my second oldest brother Alfonso. His pregnant wife was living with us and she occupied the only bedroom that did not have a dirt floor. The second baby on the way belonged to my sixteen year old brother, Manuel, who had married his fourteen year old girlfriend a few months before. They occupied one of the dirt floor bedrooms. Their dirt floor had to be wetted daily so there would not be dust flying everywhere. The third bedroom had to be shared by the rest of us. Unlike the dusty bedroom, this room was always damp since it got very little sunshine and during the rainy months the mud walls got very wet and they did not seem to dry the whole year. The only things in this room were three beds. I slept on one of these beds with my sister Catalina and my two girl cousins. Two of my brothers and my male cousin shared another. My father, mother, and youngest brother shared the third bed. My youngest brother wetted this bed. Dampness and the smell of urine permeated this room much of the time.

●

I am five years old and I am lying on the bed in our damp and pungent room. It's late in the evening and the room is dark since it has no electricity and there is only a tiny window. I am having another bad earache. It hurts so much that all I can do is lie there, crying. I am alone and I am scared because the room is so dark and my ear hurts so much. Then I see the silhouette of a woman with ample breasts come into the room. She tells me she is going to put breast milk into my aching ear. I immediately cooperate because my ear hurts so much and I am hopeful that the breast milk will make it feel better. The breast milk does not help and the pain eventually goes away.

●

It saddens me when I hear the current or former president of Mexico talk about illegal immigrants. The current president, Felipe Calderon, says the American economy needs illegal immigrants. The former president, Vicente Fox, has said many times that illegal immigrants come to this country to do the jobs that Americans do not want to do. They both say this as if they are proud of providing an uneducated, unskilled work force. Illegal immigrants risk their lives to come to America because they have no hope of a decent life in their own country. And these two presidents should be ashamed of this.

●

By the time I was about six or seven years old I already knew that I faced a lifetime of poverty and deprivation. I knew that my chances of a good education were practically zero. My father felt that girls did not have to be educated, since all they were going to do with their lives was to get married and have babies. Also, we only had one public elementary school and one small junior high school in our town. Most kids did not go to junior high because unlike elementary school, it was not free. It was actually quite expensive for most families.

My cousins did not worry about facing a lifetime of poverty or not getting a good education. They knew that once their mom saved enough money to buy a house in America – and they knew it would be soon – she would send for them to join her. Both of my sisters-in-law also felt much hope for their babies. Being unable to get a job in our town to support his pregnant wife, my sixteen year old brother, Manuel, had left for America as well. My sisters-in-law knew it was just a matter of time before they could join their husbands.

There were people in our town that did not depend on America for money or a happy life. These people were rich land owners. They sent their kids to our town's private school and took annual vacations at Mexico's beaches. Their kids drove new trucks as soon as they were old enough to drive and they wore fancy, clean, well pressed clothes. I actually knew quite a bit about their lifestyle because my second oldest sister, Josefina, married a man from a rich family.

Josefina, who as a young woman had smooth white skin, and was thin and beautiful, captivated this man. He was from a nearby ranch and his parents were rich land owners.

They moved to our town shortly after getting married and later had three children, one boy and two girls. My sister Josefina was also old enough to be my mother, so her kids were around my age. I also called them cousins. Jaime (the boy), would always tell us about their annual family vacations to various beaches.

These cousins like the other rich kids in our town went to private school. Although they played with us and were nice to us, they did not play with other poor kids. Rich kids did not play or talk with poor kids because poor kids were inferior.

As poor as I knew we were, there were kids that were even worse off. These kids walked around the town's cobblestone streets with no shoes on and they wore torn dirty clothes most of the time. Many of them did not go to school because they had to work. They worked on farms, picking fruit and planting seeds, and they also worked in town doing odd jobs.

I often wonder what happened to these kids. Did they come to America like so many people in our town? Did they work hard and possibly become successful?

•

I had no hope of going to America at a young age. My father, who worked in America for many years under the Bracero Program, did not like living there. He said he would never go back because all people did there was work. People worked all day, came home in the evening and got ready to go to work the next day. "What kind of life is that?" he would say.

My Dad loved his life in our small town. He worked as a cattle middleman, going to various farms and buying cattle. He would then sell the cattle to the local meat markets. He would eat a big breakfast in the morning, usually chile con carne (meat in chili sauce) and homemade tortillas, and come home by three o'clock for supper. He usually took a one-hour siesta after supper. Then he would go to the plaza to meet with his friends. He stayed there for hours drinking beer, smoking, and talking to his friends. I knew he would never give all this up. For me, no hope of going to America meant no hope of a decent life.

•

I decide to spend my fifty centavos weekly allowance, which I had hidden in one of Ma's plants. My brothers, sister, and cousins spend their weekly Sunday allowance money right away, but I like to save it. I like having money saved up, even if it is just a few cents and cannot buy much. "How will I spend my half peso coin?" I wonder as I walk home. I know the things I cannot buy with it; I cannot buy a bag of potato chips. My rich cousin Leticia let me have some one time. I had loved their crunchy salty taste, but they are more than a peso. I usually save my allowance for a few days, but I cannot save it for weeks. I know I will probably never be able to save up enough money to buy a Twinkie or cupcake. My cousin let me try them one time. I had never tasted anything so good before. And of course, I will not be able to buy a chocolate bar even though I always have a craving for it. The kind of chocolate I always crave is not even carried by the two small shops near our house. This chocolate comes neatly wrapped, first in silver foil and then the outer wrap. The store at the plaza carries it and it is a lot more than one peso. I sometimes wish that my cousin Leticia had never let me try it. It was so sweet and creamy unlike the chocolate Ma sometimes gives us. The kind of chocolate she gives us is used for making hot chocolate, and it is grainy, hard, and not even sweet. I am getting close to home and I finally have an idea of what I will buy, probably an apple. Ma never buys apples because they are too expensive... or maybe a jicama with chili powder on it. Those are fifty cents. A mango would be great, but they are a peso.

When I get home I see Ma talking to her friend. They are standing just inside the house and she does not acknowledge me as I pass right by them. Ma does not like to stand in front of our house gossiping, like most ladies in the neighborhood. She says it's bad for ladies to be gossiping in front of their houses, especially when they are gossiping about the people that walk by.

I am looking for my coin, but I cannot find it. The patio is my favorite place to hide my coins even though my brother, Gerardo, sometimes steals them. I like hiding them there because the patio is my favorite place in the house. The patio's mud walls, which are not painted, are covered with plants, mostly geraniums with colorful flowers. As I look for my coin, I see Ma looking at me as she tells her friend, "Rosa is not pretty like her sister Catalina or street smart like her brother Gerardo, but at least she has light skin." I stop looking for my coin and leave the house. It hurts me that Ma said those things about me when she knew I could hear her.

●

My mother was accustomed to making comparisons. After all, she had ten kids who did not behave or look alike. My mother herself had different-looking parents. Her father had blue eyes and white skin. Her mother had dark skin and Indian features. Ma had dark skin, but did not have the typical Indian features: small eyes, flat nose, high cheekbones, and full lips.

When I was a child, I heard Ma say that when she was pregnant she did not have any idea what the baby would look like. My oldest sister, Teresa, was born with dark skin, and some Indian features. My second sister, Josefina, was blond with brown eyes. My oldest and second oldest brothers looked like Teresa, but my third oldest brother, Manuel, was also blond. My other three brothers all had dark skin, but had different features. My sister, Catalina, who my mom said was the prettiest baby she ever had, was born with a head full of dark shiny black hair, white skin, and Spanish features. I was born with light skin, but with all of the Indian features.

My sister Teresa's kids, who I called my cousins, also looked different. Teresa married a man with light skin and green eyes. So, one of her daughters had green eyes, the other brown, and her son had blue eyes. They all had light skin. My sister, Josefina, married a white-looking man. Her oldest daughter, Leticia, had beautiful blue eyes and blond hair. Her son was also blond with blue eyes. Her youngest daughter had brown hair and eyes, with light skin.

Just like our family, many families in our town had very different looking kids, and comparisons were always being made. But being different was part of normal life. Therefore, we accepted our differences and lived our lives as best we could.

•

I am six years old, about to turn seven, and I cannot wait to start school. I have taught myself how to write my full name, numbers up to one hundred, and the alphabet. I do not tell anyone this because it does not matter, no one cares. Since the day Ma took me to the school to register, I have been eagerly waiting for school to start. The first day of school is everything I hoped it would be. I get a new dress, new socks, and new shoes.

I love the school as soon as I go inside. It has a clean, shiny, tile floor entrance and an open concrete center (no dirt floors anywhere). It also has a second story on one side of the school, which is something I have never seen before. The school's brick walls do not have paint peeling off like the walls in our house. I also like my teacher, a kind thin woman with short, wavy hair.

As the months go by I continue to love school. I have a couple of close friends and a few others. Some of the kids in the class are hit on their hands for talking or for not doing their homework. I always do my homework and listen to the teacher so I am never hit.

The social status of the kids in the class is very apparent. We have two doctor's daughters who are not rich enough to go to private school, but are richer than most of us. They wear different dresses every day and have shiny long hair. We also have the son of a teacher. He wears clean, well pressed slacks and shirts. There are a couple of girls who wear pretty dresses and socks with lace trim. I do not know what their dads do, but they look like they have money. A few kids come to class with messy hair and dirty clothes. Most kids do not want to sit next to these dirty kids because everyone thinks they have lice. I usually wear the same dress the whole week unless it is noticeable dirty; I am considered average like many other kids in the class.

Because I am just an average kid, I am surprised when my teacher tells me that she wants me to play the main character in a school play. The play will be performed at the school's annual Mother's Day celebration. I have attended a few of these celebrations before to watch my cousin Irma perform typical Mexican dance numbers.

The name of the play is "La Traperecita" (the little rag girl). I'm full of excitement when I get home and cannot wait to tell Ma.

Ma, I am going to be in a school play, it's called La Traperecita, I tell her.

Ma looks at me, nods, but does not say anything. I am happy anyway because I never thought I would ever be able to perform in the annual school celebration.

My cousin, Irma, performs at this celebration every year since her mom sends her money from El Norte to have the required dance dresses made for her. I have always known that my parents cannot afford to have dresses made for me. Most of the numbers performed at this event consist of various Mexican dances and the girls wear elaborate dresses. I do not remember ever seeing a play before, so for me being in a play is a very big deal.

We spend many hours practicing the play. I tell Ma she does not have to worry about getting special clothes for me. The teacher just wants me to wear my oldest dress and shoes, and to have messy hair.

The day of the event finally comes. All day I have been feeling butterflies in my stomach. I tell Ma I have to go to the school early and get ready for the play. All I need is my oldest dress since I am already wearing my oldest shoes and my hair is kind of messy. The teacher will probably make my dress look dirty and mess up my hair some more before the play. Ma seems to not have heard a thing I said because she tells me she has to comb my hair and help me change into better clothes. I tell her, no Ma I am playing a homeless girl and I do not need to have my hair combed or change into better clothes. She ignores me again and I know better than to keep arguing. So I let her comb and braid my hair, but then she goes and gets my favorite dress. This dress is from El Norte. And I really like it because it looks so new and it is bright white on top – I do not have any other bright white clothes. It is also very soft and comfortable.

I feel like crying when I get to school and my teacher looks at me. My hair is neatly braided and I am wearing a practically new dress and clean white socks. My teacher panics and tries to mess up my two braids, but Ma made them very tight so it is not possible to make them look messy and there is no time to redo them. She then looks at my dress. I tell her I told Ma that I needed to wear my oldest dress, but she would not listen to me. My kind teacher is somehow able to get patches for the dress, but when she starts hand sewing them on it, I start to cry. This is my favorite dress and I am afraid it will get ruined. She stops and I perform the play feeling sad and embarrassed – a rag girl wearing a practically new dress and socks. Why did Ma do this to me?

•

Mother is tall and thin and has long black hair. She never hugs or kisses us and she is worse to me than to

22

my brothers, sister, or cousins. I know she does not beat my brothers because boys are more valuable than girls. Someday when she gets older, they will provide financial support for her. In her eyes, daughters, who will someday depend on their husbands, will never be able to do this.

She does not beat my cousins either. She says she feels sorry for them because their dad had left them and their mom is in El Norte working hard to support them.

She does not beat my sister, Catalina, who is five years older than me and able to defend herself. But I sometimes feel that she does not get beaten because she is so pretty.

So, it is me that gets beaten. Whenever I do something wrong, I have to get on my stomach on one of the beds and Ma hits me fifteen, twenty times with a belt, up and down my back. After every beating, I hate Ma and wish that she would die. I hate her for hours even though I sort of know why she is so mean, especially to me.

Ma got married at a very young age and started having kids right away. She had a baby every other year and nursed it for as long as possible. She nursed my youngest brother, Enrique, until he was four because after him, she could no longer have babies. And Ma has to take care of so many people – my siblings and me, my cousins, my pregnant sisters-in-law, and Pa. But knowing all this does not lessen the pain she often causes me.

It was hard being a kid in Mexico, but it was also kind of fun. Most of us did not have any toys, so we spent most of our free time playing outside. We played tag and hide-and-seek almost every night. We also explored places around a nearby river and we pretended to film Mexican movies. We played cooking using leaves, sticks, and non-edible berries for most of our dishes. I enjoyed playing all those games, but my favorite game was catching crickets. A couple of times a week, we got a jar and went around the neighborhood looking for crickets. The one to catch the most crickets was the winner. Even though we had plenty of fun considering we had no toys to play with, every sixth of January (the day most kids in Latin America hope to receive a toy from the Three Wise Men – no Santa Claus for Mexican kids) we went to bed hoping that in the morning there would be a toy next to our shoe.

Most years, my siblings, cousins, and I did not get any toys. But when I was seven, I got the most beautiful doll I had ever seen. My doll was big, soft, and she had a colorful, pretty dress with a lace trim collar. She also had soft white socks and black shoes. I was so happy. I had gotten a doll before, but not like this one. The other doll was small and hard, and her legs and arms could not be bent.

I played with my new the doll the whole day and was looking forward to playing with it the next day. But at the end of the day, my mother took my doll away. She said that I would get it again on the next Sixth of January. I pleaded, begged, and cried, but my doll was taken away anyway. I had to wait a year to get it again and a year seemed like an eternity to me.

As promised, I got the doll back the following year, only for it to be taken away again at the end of the day.

The next year I was nine years old, not interested in playing with dolls anymore. I told Ma I did not want the doll anymore, so it stayed locked up in Ma's dresser. For years to come, it was painful to think about my beautiful doll and how I only played with it for two days.

•

It is about nine in the evening and for the first time I will be taking part in the annual pilgrimage to a church in a nearby town. I have been waiting for years to be part of this annual event. I am now seven years old and can finally participate. We are supposed to walk from the edge of town for about six hours, starting at midnight, and continue walking until we reach Salamanca. Once we make it to this town, we need to walk some more to a very special church, attend Mass, and spend the rest of the day having fun shopping. At the end of the day we are to come back by bus.

It's finally midnight and we start walking. There are about twenty people in our group. My mother, sisters, and cousins are here. Even my youngest brother, who is only six, is here. He did not want to be left behind, so Ma let him come.

The road that will take us to Salamanca is a dirt road with lots of little rocks on it. I cannot really see the rocks, but I can feel myself stepping on them. I am enjoying walking in the dark and barely being able to see the trees, and wheat and corn fields along the road.

I start getting bored and look around for someone to talk to. I see one of my real cousins close by and catch up to her.

Do you like the walk? I ask.

I am too tired to talk, she says to me.

I still want to talk to someone as I walk, so I go over to Ma. She is talking to her friend and completely ignores me. I move away from her and start to think of ways I can entertain myself. I count trees, but after a while this also gets boring. I then decide to close my eyes and see what it feels like to walk in complete darkness. At first I only close them for a few seconds. Then I get more daring and keep them closed for much longer. Suddenly my foot is cold and wet and I realize I am falling into the nearby creek. I cannot keep myself from falling in. The water feels cold and muddy and the fast moving current is carrying me away from the people up above, who are screaming. I know quite a few people have drowned in this creek so I grab on to branches to keep my face above the water. Suddenly, I feel some one grabbing me and realize it is my little brother who has jumped in to save me. My little brother knows how to swim, but he is only six and I wish he had not jumped in. I lose consciousness and when I come back I am out of the water, freezing, and all muddy. I find out that my second oldest sister, Josefina, jumped in to rescue my brother and me. I am relieved when I see my brother next to me. He looks cold and muddy, but he is already talking about what happened. I tell everyone I closed my eyes when I was walking because I was so bored. Ma gets mad at me for being so stupid and stays mad the whole day even though I almost died.

•

Years later, I wondered why that night I kept walking towards the creek not realizing that I was so close to it. I got my answer at about age sixteen, when I went to see a doctor for the first time. I was having another earache, like the many I had had since early childhood. But now I could go see a doctor since I had a part-time job and what, to me, was plenty of money. The doctor and his assistant cleaned my ears and an unbelievable amount of earwax came out, as well as small cotton balls that the doctor said had probably been in my ears since I was a very young child. He had never seen anything like it in all his years in practice.

As I walked home that day, I was amazed and relieved. I was amazed that cars could make so much noise and was relieved that the reason I failed the

hearing tests given at school every year was not really
a hearing problem.

●

Normally I do not mind the weekly baths even though they are quite a production. I like feeling clean and being able to put on clean clothes. We take our baths in a giant pot-like container on Saturday nights, using a bucket of clean warm water, which we use to wet and rinse ourselves. The water is usually warmed up on the stove and since we do not have a bathroom we put the pot in our bedroom. I hate taking baths towards the end because by that time the giant pot is filled with dirty water. Most of the time, I am able to give myself a bath with some help from my older sister.

Sometimes Ma gives me a bath which is the case on one particular occasion. Instead of warming up the water on the stove, she puts the container outside. She tells me to put some water in it and to let the water warm up in the sun. It's Sunday afternoon and I need to have a bath before our weekly Sunday night Mass. I do not like taking baths outside, but do not complain because no one else is in the house. My sisters-in-law stay with their parents on Sundays and all the kids are out doing something.

When I am finally being given my bath, I realize that the front door is open and I am right in front of it —

completely naked. I am not that close to the door, but I recognize every person walking by.

Ma, can you please close the front door? People can see me when they walk by. I am so embarrassed.

Ah, no, Ma says.

I start crying. Please Ma, can you please close the door? I do not want people to see me naked, specially, *chiquillos* (boys) and men."

No, Ma says again.

I plead, beg, but Ma never closes the door.

•

Our school is having a free magic show for the kids in our small town. Ma knows about this show and that we all want to see it. Nevertheless, shortly before we have to leave for the show, she tells me I have to go to a store – which is not nearby – to get something she needs for supper. I complain about having to go since the show will be starting soon. I have to go anyway, so I hurry up hoping to still be able to see most of the show. I arrive at the store, only to find out that they are out of the item Ma needs. Quickly I return home and tell Ma the store does not have what she needs. She tells me to go to another store. I refuse. I do not want to miss the show. I am beaten badly for being defiant and have to go get what she needs, crying all the way to the store.

•

My Dad refers to me as "mi niña" (my little girl), or Rosita – not Rosa like everyone else. Supposedly, I am his favorite because I look just like his mother – small eyes, high cheekbones, and full lips. Sometimes after dinner he sets me up on his lap and bounces me a few times. My siblings make fun of me for being treated like such a baby. I do not care. In my eyes they are just jealous. Unfortunately, the job he has, buying cattle from nearby farms and selling it to our local meat markets, keeps him out of the house most of the day.

Papa – as I like to call him – never went to school a day in his life and does not know how to read or write, yet he is the leader of a group of peasants trying to get farm land from the government. He goes to Mexico City often to lobby for the peasants. One time he even met with the Mexican president. As much as I love my father, I know he has many flaws.

I often wonder why he lets my brother Gerardo, who is eight years old, hang out with guys twice his age, drink beer, and smoke cigarettes with them.

I can hear the anguish in my mother's voice when she asks my older brother, Julian, to go look for him and bring him home. I can also hear the pain in her voice when she asks my brother not to hang out with such good-for-nothing guys. She begs him not to drink or smoke, but my brother, who is very skinny from skipping so many meals, never listens to her. I never see father talk to him or punish him for his bad behavior. He never goes looking for him when it is supper time and my brother is nowhere to be seen.

Although Father neglects Gerardo, he is nice to the rest of us. He brings us ripe, delicious fruits – whenever he can – from the farms he went to that day, especially, watermelon, which we love. He never complains about how far he has to walk carrying the juicy fruits. And he never beats us. I was six years old when I saw Father being violent for the first time.

He is home after a heavy night of drinking. His long-sleeved white shirt is unbuttoned and his round belly is sticking out. His small eyes are red and they make him look scary. He starts yelling at Ma. All of us kids get so frightened that we jump on the bed with her. It's a weekend, so my sisters-in-law are not home. We are all on the bed with Ma when Papa comes in with a rusty old machete threatening to kill her. Ma calls him a coward. Why don't you ever do this when my older sons are here from El Norte? she yells.

Why does Ma say that to him, I wonder, when he has a machete in his hand? Papa gets more enraged. He starts moving the machete side to side coming towards us. I jump out of bed and hug him. I am crying, shaking, hugging his legs, which is as far as my arms can reach, while he is still moving the machete above me. I know in my heart that he will not hurt me. He eventually puts the machete away and we all sleep with Ma that night, all eight of us.

31

From then on, every time we find out he is getting drunk, we hide the machete. Unfortunately, later on after another night of heavy drinking, he once again threatens to kill Ma, this time with a butcher knife. On this night I do not run over to him and no one tries to calm him down. We just stay in bed with Ma, crying, shaking, and protecting her. The next time he is out drinking all night, we hide all the knives as well.

For years after that, when he came home drunk and tried to hurt Ma or my sister, who he was sometimes mad at, my siblings and I cried and held his fists and he would stop.

I always forgave Father for what he put us through. I knew that he was not really himself when he was drunk and he never actually hurt anyone. He would never hurt any of us or our mother, I believed. After all he had never even spanked me.

When I was eight years old I realized how wrong I had been.

•

It was around eight when I came home that evening. I had been playing tag with the neighborhood kids. Where is Ma? I asked, since at this time she was usually putting together a small meal for us before going to bed. She is in the bedroom resting; she does not feel good, I was told.

Ma slept alone that night, all covered up. Enrique, my youngest brother, had to sleep on an already crowded bed, which was shared by my two older brothers and cousin. Father slept on the floor right outside our dirt floor bedroom.

The next day we all saw our mother. Her face was unrecognizable, black eyes, swollen face, and lips twice the regular size. She also had bruises on her body. I had seen bruises on her before, but I always assumed she had bumped into something or that one of the cows Father sometimes brought home had kicked her. I knew cows were mean.

Later that day, I found out what happened. Father beat Ma because when he came home, he saw her talking to our neighbor, a man in his forties, who lived with his mom and brother. They were just talking through our very high cactus fence. Father was not drunk when he beat her and I realized then that my father often beat Ma when there was no one around to protect her.

After that horrible beating Ma hardly ever spoke to my father. And it seemed that the only time she was happy was when she received a letter from El Norte or when one of my brothers actually came home from there.

Also, after that beating Ma did not seem to care about the rumors that whenever my father went to Mexico City – and stayed there for days – he stopped along the way to see his other woman, whom supposedly he had kids with. She also seemed glad that Pa was usually gone on weekends. Being very friendly and a good dancer, he was always invited to wedding receptions taking place at nearby ranchos. And Ma did not care that many people in the Pueblo looked up to Papa because when he met with the Mexican president, Papa talked to him as if he had known him for a long time.

•

About once a month, Ma goes to the post office to pick up a letter from El Norte, usually from my sister Teresa. Every letter she gets includes a money order and occasionally some dollar bills for the kids, sent to us by our older brothers. Whenever I get a dollar bill, all I want to do is hold it. The bill feels so thick and crisp, unlike the Mexican peso bills which are thin, dirty, and wrinkled. Even though I want to hold on to this beautiful money for a long time, it is not long before I go to the bank to cash it.

The money Teresa sends is supposed to be for the support of her three kids, but we all benefit from it. Every time Ma gets a remittance, she and Teresa's oldest daughter, Irma, go to Irapuato, a nearby city, to buy food and some other badly needed items.

Whenever they go, all the kids complain because Ma always takes Irma. I often feel that Irma is Ma's favorite child, even though she is only her granddaughter. After I complain countless times Ma eventually takes me.

It's my first time going to a city and I have never seen shops with tall glass windows. I try to go through one thinking there is nothing there and I bump my head on it. Ma laughs at me and when we come home, she tells everyone what I did, even though I had asked her not to.

●

Every other year or so, Teresa also sends a box of clothes. These are clothes that no longer fit the kids she cares for. Even though my cousins always get to pick clothes first, I am happy to get whatever they do not like or which does not fit them. My sister, Catalina, does not like picking clothes last, so she sometimes does not get any clothes. She often tries to convince me not to take the leftovers, but I cannot resist going through the few clothing items left after my cousins have gone through them. To me, every item coming from El Norte is beautiful.

Sometimes one of my brothers living in El Norte brings the boxes and he also brings with him toothpaste, toothbrushes, lotions, and fragrant creamy soaps – items that we can never afford.

When we get our toothbrushes we do not know how to use them since we only get them every few years. We do not have any sinks in the house, so we have to use one of the two faucets in the patio. The faucets sit low and we have to bend down to rinse our mouths. I like to wait until my brothers are finished brushing their teeth because they always try to spit the water from their mouths onto my feet and my girl cousin's feet. We brush our teeth for a couple of weeks until the toothpaste runs out.

I love it when my brothers come even when they do not bring anything, as is the case when they are deported and even though they make fun of my brother Enrique and me because we often have runny noses. Since there are no paper products in the house to wipe our noses with – no tissue, napkins, paper towels or toilet paper – all we can do is snort back the mucus.

When either Manuel or Alfonso comes, Papa does not become violent. And when they talk about El Norte, we all sit around them trying to imagine such a wonderful place. In El Norte, they say, we live in apartments that have a bathroom with a toilet and shower. We have color televisions, a refrigerator, and all kinds of furniture. In the United States, they have huge grocery stores where we can buy whatever kind of food we want and they have many free schools where we go to learn English. I love listening to my brothers talk about El Norte.

My oldest brother, Jose, who does not have a wife and kids in Mexico, only comes one time. He has no choice but to come home because when he is deported, he is sent so far south into Mexico that he cannot sneak right back across the border. Jose hates coming to a place with no jobs, no bathrooms, and very few food choices.

•

It's Sunday, my favorite day of the week. I love Sundays for many reasons. On this day the house is very quiet, since my sisters-in-law go spend the day at their parents' houses. Also, this day is quite festive in our pueblo. It is the day when people put on their best clothes and go to the plaza to eat, talk to friends, and listen to music. It is also our Church day.

I really like how clean I feel on this day, as we can only bathe once a week. But what I love the most about Sundays is being able to wear a dress from El Norte. I like the way the dresses feel – so soft and comfortable – and I like showing them off when we go to the plaza and to church.

As much as I like Sundays, there is one thing I hate. Most Sundays, we have beef soup for supper. I hate the greasy taste of this soup and eating the meat is even worse. The meat is actually mostly fat, meat with little or no fat is too expensive. I know better than to complain, so I eat the soup feeling like I am going to vomit every time I put a spoonful in my mouth. I have to finish my bowl of soup every single time.

•

When it comes to food, my favorite day is Good Friday. This is the only day of the year when kids' stomachs are so full that you can see them sticking out. On this day Ma makes beans like she does most days except Sundays, but she also makes ground shrimp patties in some kind of red sauce and sliced cactus to go with them. She cooks lentils and a delicious thick yellow soup. And this is the only day when she makes dessert, fruit salad with watermelon, oranges, bananas and lettuce – my favorite food. She also slices Mexican rolls, fries them, and covers them in a *piloncillo* (brown sugar and cinnamon) sauce – most kids' favorite food. Good Friday culminates a week of attending live Stations of the Cross, daily Masses, and the reenactment of Jesus' crucifixion. But for most kids, it's the only day of the year when we eat an enjoyable meal.

•

Sometimes on Saturday mornings, Ma does not cook breakfast because Pa brings home a cow's head for us to eat. On these mornings, all the kids sit around the table and anxiously wait for Papa to unwrap the cow's head which is always wrapped in off-white, thick paper. As soon as Ma puts the warm tortillas on the table all the kids want to get the warm tender meat that used to be the cow's cheeks, but Pa makes us take turns grabbing the meat.

Papa never eats this part of the head. He says the eyeballs are more nourishing and he always eats them first. When all the meat from the cheeks and the rest of the head is gone, Pa opens up the brain, our second favorite part, and puts some of this mushy whitish part of the head on our tortilla. Before eating our brain taco we put a little bit of salt on it. Pa tells us when we are done with our taco we will be a little bit smarter. We all believe him.

●

I come home to find boxes of tomatoes stacked near the front of the house and find out that Papa got all the boxes from a farmer who could not pay him. We have to eat them before they go bad, one of my brothers tells me. I am so happy to hear that. I love tomatoes, but Ma only buys two or three a day to make chili con carne for Papa. I eat about ten a day for a couple weeks. They are so big, sweet, and juicy. Everyone else complains about having to eat them.

Once the tomatoes are gone, we go back to having no food to eat in between meals and back to having fresh vegetables as treats only occasionally.

●

Since we do not have a refrigerator, Ma goes to the plaza every morning to shop for whatever she needs to make breakfast and supper. She does not have to worry about a third meal because at night we just have Mexican bread or leftovers from our three o'clock meal. She only gets twenty pesos a day from Papa to shop for food, so there is never enough money to buy any treats.

A few times a year we go to a local farm to buy carrots and eat them fresh. The rest of the time we eat them cooked in some kind of soup. We also have cucumbers and lettuce a few times a year. Once a year we are able to buy cooked sweet potatoes when they are in season. We all walk to a stand near the plaza, carrying our own plates, and buy sweet delicious sweet potatoes. I often wonder why Ma cannot cook them herself.

When these vegetables are not available, the only vegetables we can eat are cabbage and jalapeño peppers. I do not like cabbage and jalapeño peppers are too hot for me.

Even though we have very limited food choices my siblings, cousins, and I seldom get sick. And we all have perfect teeth except for my cousin Carmen, who lives with us. She is the only one in the family with crooked teeth.

Like most of the kids in the Pueblo, we never go see a doctor when we do get sick. If we have a stomach ache, we are given herbal tea. If we have a bad cold or the flu, we stay in bed.

•

Ma, her sister, a couple of cousins, and I are walking to a nearby farm to buy vegetables. All of a sudden my stomach starts hurting. The pain is getting more intense and I don't think I can keep walking, I tell Ma. It must be that hernia of yours, she says. She takes me behind some bushes. You need to pee and drink some of it. It will make your stomach ache go away, she tells me. I do not want to drink my pee, but my stomach hurts so much and I do not know what else to do. So I drink the pee hoping the pain will go away. It does not, and we continue walking to the farm.

Some of my siblings, cousins, and I get this skin condition spreading among the kids in the pueblo. At first we get blisters all over our legs and arms. They itch so much, but we are not allowed to touch them.

Our neighbors, a mom and her grown daughters, feel sorry for us. They tell us to go to their house so they can put ointment on us to stop the itching. They put ointment on us until the blisters turn into scabs and they do not itch anymore.

Even though we have two doctors' offices in our town, the only contact most kids in the pueblo have with medical staff is when they open the town's clinic for free mandatory shots. About every other year we go to the clinic and get in long lines for our shots.

We do not have a dentist in the pueblo. Since candy and sodas are too expensive for most families, we do not seem to need one.

•

Once every few years, two of my real cousins come to visit from El Norte. Ma's sister, Maria, was married to their father, Rafael, until she passed away from cancer. My cousins are my older brothers' age, so their kids are my age. Their kids were all born in the United States and their Spanish sounds funny.

When they come, they stay with Rafael who lives across the street. He runs a small shop out of his house and most kids in the neighborhood call him Tio (Uncle). Ma tells us not to call him Tio, even though he was married to her sister for many years. She says kids call him Tio hoping he will give them a free treat when he is in a good mood. These kids have no pride and will do anything for free candy, she tells us.

It is the late sixties and there are very few families coming from El Norte. When these families come to visit, everyone in the pueblo knows it. They dress as nice, if not nicer, than the rich people in the pueblo. The kids wear clean, wrinkle-free clothes every day. The girls run around with us wearing shiny, patent leather shoes. All the kids in the neighborhood envy them.

A heavy-set lady who was raised by my Ma's sister, Maria, also comes to visit. She is my cousin's step sister. When she comes, she brings her family as well. They are not really related to us, but are very nice to us nonetheless. Ma says that her sister, a saint, treated her husband's kids as her own, so they feel obligated to treat us with respect.

I like it when they come. The daughters, all teenagers, are thin and pretty and have shiny black hair. They call one of them "Rosie". I wish I could look like her and be called Rosie instead of Rosa.

•

Every family or person that comes from El Norte always goes back except for one, Manuela la loca (crazy Manuela) she is called. Ma tells us how she came back from El Norte years ago, wearing a fur coat, fancy clothes, styled hair, and well done makeup. She had to come back from El Norte because she was going crazy. Ma felt very sorry for her because every year she seemed to get worse.

Now this once-elegant beautiful woman roams the streets barefoot and wearing a torn, dirty black dress. Her once-styled hair now gets chopped off often. She roams the streets talking to herself and staying away from people. She poops on an area called La Orilla, at the end of our block. It is called La Orilla because it is where the pueblo ends. Some people even throw their garbage there because it is just empty land. She relieves herself there even if people are watching, but barks at them if they stare. All the neighborhood kids are afraid of her, but yell at her "Manuela la loca" when she is not too close.

I am afraid of her as well, but I also feel sorry for her. How could this have happened to her? What if someday I make it to El Norte as she did and go crazy too?

●

Ma wishes she was raised in the United States. She tells us how her father worked on a farm in the United States for a number of years when she and her siblings were little. The farm owner really liked him and told him he should bring his family north. He would help them get papers.

Why didn't my father listen to his boss? She sadly remarks when she tells us the story, and she adds, my life would be so different.

●

It is mid-morning and there is much commotion in the house. My fifteen year-old sister-in-law, Lola, is having her first baby. All the kids in the house have gathered outside her dirt floor bedroom, next to the patio, to hear everything that is going on. Earlier in the morning Ma rushed out of the house to get the mid-wife. Now we hear them talking and my sister-in-law screaming. We have never heard a baby being born, so we wait for hours until we hear the baby cry. A healthy baby boy is born and Lola and Ma name him Toni. His father, Manuel, is far away working in El Norte. At sixteen years of age he had to go join my other two brothers, so he could get a job and support his expectant wife.

After Toni is born, my brother sends money to Lola more often. When Toni gets older we are able to have some of his treats if we take care of him. My sister, cousins, and I want to take care of him all the time so we can have some of his crackers, apple pieces, and bananas.

The whole neighborhood seems to like Toni. My sister-in-law dresses him better than most of the one year-olds on the block and he seems to always be happy, unlike other toddlers in the neighborhood who do not have their dad working up north.

Toni's father, Manuel, comes to have him baptized. I do not remember ever being to a Baptism, but I know how they are celebrated and it is hard to wait for this special day.

Baptisms take place at the church next to the plaza on Saturdays, the same day as weddings, Confirmations, and Communions. Everyone puts on their best clothes and goes to the church. After the Mass, all the kids surround the godfather for the *bolo* (coin throwing). The godfather tosses many handfuls of coins on top of the kids. Sometimes when I am walking to my sister's house I see boys near the front of the church, leaning on the wall with their hands in their pockets waiting for the Baptism Mass to end so they can participate in the *bolo*.

I have never seen a girl waiting there and I would never go to a bolo either unless I was invited. I have never seen my brothers waiting for the bolo, but I assume that sometimes they do.

Another good thing about a Baptism is the ice cream and cookies served in the evening. Again, there are kids that go to have ice cream and cookies even though they are not invited. Ma does not allow us to do this and says that kids who go to someone else's celebration have no shame.

Manuel stays for a few weeks after Toni's Baptism and then goes back to his job in El Norte, leaving his wife pregnant again. He has no problem crossing the border illegally.

•

Months after Lola has her first baby, my other sister-in-law, Amelia, has her first baby – a healthy baby boy with very light skin. She names him Armando. When he gets older we all want to carry him because his is such a lovely baby.

Ma is very proud of her new grandchildren and compliments my sisters-in-laws for taking such good care of their babies, unlike other moms in the neighborhood who walk around carrying dirty, smelly babies.

My brother Alfonso, who always sent the most money to his wife, sends even more money after the baby is born. Ma says he is a very hard worker and does not like to waste money.

Months later, Amelia, buys all kinds of food for Armando, now a toddler and hides it in her bedroom. On weekends, when she goes to her parents' house, we go in her room and look for the food we know she has hidden. Usually we find apples, crackers, and other goodies.

When she comes back all the food is gone, but she does not reprimand us. She knows we only get two and a half meals a day and that we are always hungry for snacks.

Alfonso comes to see his new son and brings a box full of clothes for everyone. Other than my baby brother, Enrique, Alfonso is my favorite, even though he always seems to find ways of making fun of my baby brother and me. When he makes fun of us, it is as if he feels sorry for us, unlike my brother Manuel who calls us *mensos* (dumb), *mugrosos* (dirty), and tells us to stay away from him.

When Alfonso goes back to El Norte, he leaves his wife pregnant again.

●

It is mid-January and everyone is getting ready for our annual festival. We call it La Fiesta. It lasts ten days and it's the only time of the year when rich and poor people have fun together. It is supposed to be all about celebrating our town's saint, Santa Candelaria, but I as well as all the other kids mainly care about the rides and the nightly fireworks show.

It is the first day of La Fiesta and my cousins and I are wearing new shoes and new dresses from El Norte. I do not have a new dress for each day like some girls, but I am happy I have a new dress for the first and the final day. My brothers are wearing new clothes too. We first go to Mass, everyone in the pueblo seems to be there wearing their best clothes. The church is very crowded and we have to stand outside. I can hardly hear the priest and I can barely see our beloved saint. She looks so beautiful with her white skin and light brown hair. She is holding her baby, who looks just like her, and she is wearing a gold crown and a light blue dress with gold trim and a gold rope around the waist.

After the Mass, our saint is put on a wood base and carried from the church by the plaza to our other church about three blocks away; everyone who was at the Mass follows her. She will stay at the other church until the festival is over. For the next nine days we will be coming to this church to celebrate Mass. As we leave the church I cannot help but notice how out of place Santa Candelaria looks in this church. The whole church is made out of gray rocks and all you see when you look at the walls are gray rocks. The church has no benches or paintings of saints and angels like our other church. Our saint with her blue dress and gold crown is the only bright thing in the whole church.

When the Mass is over, it is time for rides, music, eating and shopping. For over a week I have been seeing rides being put together, but now I cannot decide which one to go on first. I only have enough money for a few rides so I have to choose carefully. All the rides look old and rusty and make funny noises. They have metal seats with paint peeling off and I wonder if any of them will break while I am on them. I finally get on one that turns me upside down and I have not been so happy in a long time.

After a couple rides I see my cousin Carmen and we go on a couple more rides together. I do not get along with her most of the time, but I have not seen my best friend all day and I do not want to go on another ride alone. After the rides we go and look at all the stuff different people are selling. Near the plaza, vendors have set up tent-like shops selling handmade clothing, toys, and leather items. Beyond those tents are vendors selling ceramic dishes, pots, and mugs. The vendors selling the ceramics have all their stuff on the ground and it is hard to walk on the street because they occupy both sides of the street and there are a lot of people strolling and shopping. Carmen and I spot miniature dishes and pots and we cannot wait to find Ma and beg for money to buy them. We finally find her and she tells us we will be able to get some before La Fiesta is over.

There are people selling all kinds of foods and the smell makes us hungry, but we know we cannot eat until we are finished with the rides. After the rides we go looking for my sister Catalina or my brother Julian to see if they will buy some food for us. It is nighttime now and there is no use looking for Ma. She is probably back at home and we do not want to walk all the way home. We find Julian and he buys us hotcakes. I love hotcakes and I hope I can eat them every day since this is the only time of the year when people make them.

After eating there is nothing to do but wait for the Castillo to be lit up. The Castillo is a structure almost as tall as a house but only a few yards wide, so it does not take long for the fireworks show to end. Music has been playing at the plaza since the Mass ended and it will be nice to go home where it is nice and quiet. My sister Catalina, my cousin Irma, and my brother Julian, will probably stay here until midnight. Next to the main plaza there is another plaza called, El Jardin (the garden). This is where everyone over twelve years of age and not married spends the night. The girls walk around the center of the Jardin holding hands with each other. The boys and men stand around watching them, waiting for the ones they like to give a flower to and throw confetti at them. Catalina is very proud of the fact that she gets more flowers than almost anyone else in the Pueblo.

•

It is the early seventies and not too many people from the Pueblo are in El Norte. Yet everyone seems to know at least someone coming from there for our annual festival. When they come, families seem happier and the town becomes even more alive, thanks to the extra money brought or sent from the United States for the special celebration.

I only know a few people coming from there, but I can tell who else is coming to visit by the way they dress. They wear clean pressed clothes and shiny new dress shoes all the time – not just when they go to the Plaza – like the rich people in the pueblo. But unlike the rich people, they hang out with ordinary people and stay in their mud-brick houses with no bathrooms.

When I walk by the plaza, I see them buying perros calientes and hamburgesas (hot dogs and hamburgers) at the only place in the pueblo that sells them. Then when La Fiesta is over, every person that came to visit from El Norte leaves, taking with them siblings, cousins, or friends. They will help them travel north and then help them cross the border illegally.

By this time it is very apparent that the pueblo's population decreases after every festival. At the same time, the festival gets bigger every year with more people from El Norte coming to visit. They bring money for more rides, music groups, confetti throwing, and religious events.

•

Ma hands me a grayish old container and tells me I need to go buy two liters of milk. You have to go to the house near your school, she says. We have to try a different place for milk because the people we buy milk from now are putting water in it. Their milk is so watery. How can they think we would not notice?

I was at the house near our school once before to buy milk and saw the best looking non-rich boy I had ever seen. I did not remember ever seeing him at school before, even though we have a pretty small school. I had really liked his head full of shiny black hair and light skin. He looked so clean and well mannered.

As I am walking, feeling the stones of our cobblestone street under my worn shoes, I think about how I look and wonder if that boy will be there. I wish I was not wearing trensas (braids), only the peasant-looking girls and women in the pueblo wear them. The rich girls never wear trensas and most girls, including my sister and cousins, only wear them once in a while.

Ma insists on braiding my hair because it is long and she does not want it to get all tangled. I wish my hair looked the way it looks on Sundays, clean, shiny, and unbraided. I also wish I was not wearing this wrinkled dress which I have worn and slept in for days. I'm supposed to take off my dress before going to bed and sleep in my slip, but most of the time I sleep in my clothes because there is no place to hang them and they will get all wrinkled anyway. Besides, we have only one cover on the bed I share with my sister and cousins and when I sleep in my slip I always get cold.

When I arrive at the house I do not see the boy there and I am thankful for that since I look so bad. The milk is in a bottle-like container that reaches my waist and I think Ma will be happy because it looks thick and creamy. I wonder where they keep their cows since the house smells so clean and I only see a few flies.

As the milk is being poured into my container by a tall man, I see the boy come in. We stare at each other for a few seconds. By the way he is staring at me I can tell he does not mind my trensas or my wrinkled dress. I feel myself blushing and I cannot wait to pay for the milk so I can leave.

When school resumes in the fall, I cannot believe my eyes when I see him in class sitting a couple of rows away from me. I find out that his family moved to the Pueblo over the summer, but that they are not planning on staying long. I like him, but he makes me nervous and I think it will be better if they do not stay in the Pueblo very long.

•

Every couple of months I go to a pharmacy near the plaza to buy cold cream. This is my favorite errand. I like it when the clerk brings out a very large container full of creamy fragrant cold cream and puts it into my small container. I wish I could stick my hand into the large plastic container and know what the white cream really feels like, since at home I can only use a little bit of cold cream on Sundays after my weekly bath. I cannot use the cold cream during the week even if my skin looks dry and ashy.

•

I am eight years-old and I will be having my First Communion in a few days. I am not looking forward to it even though I have been preparing for it for a couple of years by attending catechism classes.

My cousin Carmen will be having it at the same time and she is not happy either. In fact, she is angry about having it at the same time as me.

Her mom, Teresa, sent her money from El Norte so that our neighbor, a seamstress, could make a beautiful princess-like dress for her. My cousin really wanted a dress like that. But Ma said it would not be right for her to have a beautiful Communion dress when I was having a very plain dress made for me because we have no money.

The day of our First Communion comes. As we are walking to the church I am thankful that the Mass is early in the morning and only a few people are out on the street. My cousin is mad at me because we had identical dresses made for us. Our dresses are made from satin, but with no fancy details. They are similar to our regular dresses, only longer and all white. I think my cousin looks good. She is very short and the plain long dress makes her look taller.

I think I look horrible. I am the tallest girl in the group and I am so skinny. I think the dress makes me look like the long white candle that I am holding. When we get to the church, we see all the other girls wearing puffy, princess-like dresses, and this makes my cousin even madder. I feel so embarrassed I wish I could disappear. I look like a tall white stick among all the girls.

My sister Josefina is my Godmother and I am not happy about that either. I wanted someone else to be my Godmother, anyone but my sister Josefina. I do not know why Ma picked her. Josefina always invites my sister Catalina to her house, calls her Catita, gives her clothes, and says how pretty she is. She never invites me or gives me clothes, and she tells me I got my unattractive Indian features from Papa's mom – whom she knew.

After the Communion Mass, we walk back home. The streets are more crowded now and I see some people staring. I want to walk faster, but I can't because it's hard walking in new dress shoes.

When we get home I want to take my dress off and wear my favorite dress from El Norte, but Ma will not let me. She is preparing a special meal and inviting relatives over.

The meal is the only thing I have been looking forward to. For months Ma has been raising turkeys in our backyard for this meal. She killed them yesterday by cutting off their heads. It was sad seeing the turkeys run for a few seconds after their heads were cut off.

We will be having *mole* with turkey and Spanish rice. I love this meal, which people only make on special occasions like Baptisms, Communions, and weddings.

My cousin does not care for the meal and just wants this day to end. Her sister Irma adds to her anger by reminding her that she had a princess dress adorned with lace and beads for her First Communion. And my sister Catalina tells her it's a shame that she had to wear such an ugly dress when she could have had a beautiful one made for her with the money her Mom sent from El Norte.

Why do you have to cause Carmen more grief? I want to say to my sister, but I am too chicken. Also, I want Carmen to forget it's my fault she could not have the dress she wanted.

●

It was not the first time my sister caused someone grief. My brother Enrique and I always stayed away from her because she always called us bugger face, dummies, and *mugrosos* (dirty kids) among other names. My brother Gerardo, who is two years older than I, was not afraid of her anymore. One time when she went after him with her long nails, he punched her so hard that she landed on the ground. From then on she

56

left him alone and had even more time to harass my brother Enrique and I.

Catalina usually left my cousins alone, but once in a while she would fight with my cousin Irma. With her shiny black hair, white skin, small lips, pointy nose, and perfectly proportioned body, she was one of the prettiest girls in the pueblo. By the time she was eleven she already had a boyfriend and other boys after her. This contributed greatly to her attitude and mean spirit.

On a regular basis she was seen talking to and kissing her boyfriends on the corner of our block. This infuriated my father and he would go get her and bring her home. It bewildered me how she would make Father so mad on purpose. Catalina also disobeyed Ma constantly and made faces at her when she was told to do her chores.

●

I am in second grade and I am trying to memorize a long speech about one of the leaders of the Mexican Revolution. I am supposed to do this speech at the annual Mother's Day celebration. I cannot believe that my teacher chose me for the speech. I do well in her class, but there are many other students who are less shy than me and I think she should have given it to one of them. Nevertheless, in a way I am happy that she has confidence in me.

When Catalina sees me practicing the speech, she tells me that I will mess up on the day of the event. She keeps telling me this every chance she gets. The day of the event finally arrives and I am at the microphone. I say the first part of the speech, but then I start to sweat and tremble. All I can think about is my sister telling me that I am going to mess up, and I forget the rest of the speech.

A year or so later, I am asked by my teacher to carry the Mexican flag at a monthly school assembly. When my sister sees me practicing with a stick at home, she knows what I will be doing and tells me I will mess up. I will not let Catalina get to me again, I tell myself when the teacher gives me the flag. Then I have fun parading the flag around the school accompanied by a classmate on each side.

•

It is late in the afternoon when I realize I only have one sheet of paper left in my homework notebook and I need more than one sheet to finish my homework. I have no choice but to go ask Ma for money so I can buy a new notebook. I ask Ma if I can have some money. She says, how can I have money when your father only gives me twenty pesos a day and that is barely enough for food? She adds, I am sure your father is in the plaza. Go there and ask him for money. Make sure when you ask him his friends can hear you so he will have no choice but to give you the money. He always has money for beer and cigarettes, and wants his friends to believe he has money for everything his family needs as well.

As I walk toward the plaza I start getting an upset stomach. Pa has told us many times not to ask him for money when he is at the plaza with his friends. But what am I supposed to do? I need to finish my homework. I know he always carries a lot of money in his pocket, but that's the money he will need the next day when he goes to the farms to buy cattle. In a way I hope I do not find him. I know I will get in trouble at school if I don't finish my homework, but I hate making Papa upset. I find him very easily and I have no choice but to ask him for the money. When I ask him he pulls out a stack of money. He always keeps the big bills on the outside – to show off Ma says – so it takes him a few seconds to get to the one peso bills. He does not seem upset at all when he gives me the money, but I know he will give me a hard time later.

●

Irma, Carmen, and I start feeling painful pinching and itchiness on our heads and right away we know why. We have lice. One of us must have gotten lice at school and since we sleep together they spread to the other two. We wonder why Catalina does not have lice for she sleeps with us too.

We always knew it was just a matter of time before one of us caught lice somewhere. At school we tried to stay away from girls who came to school with messy hair. We just knew they had lice. When we were in line buying tortillas, we tried not to be too close to girls with uncombed, dirty hair.

For the next couple of days I sit in class looking at the girls with the messy hair wondering if one of them gave me the lice. I am also trying not to scratch my itchy head because I do not want anyone to know what I have on my head. I always pay attention in class, but my head itches so much all I think about is going home, undoing my trensas, and scratching my head for a long, long time. I do not want my best friend to know of my condition, so I cannot even scratch when I am with her.

Every day now when we come home from school, we have to have someone pick our heads and look for the pests. We sit on the hard ground in the patio and Catalina, who does not have lice, goes through Irma's head and takes out the lice and their eggs. Irma picks through my head, and I have to do the same with Carmen. The bugs are black and I can spot them because Carmen's hair is brown. I squish them and blood comes out of them. The eggs are white and make a popping sound when I press on them with my thumb nails.

My sister, Josefina, found out that we have lice and will not let her daughters come to our house to play. She does not want us to go to her house either. She says her daughters have never had lice and it would be embarrassing sending them to their private school with lice on their heads. No one there has lice.

We get rid of the pests and their eggs before they spread to other people in the house and I am thankful for that since I hated picking them out of Carmen's head. It was not so bad, though, picking them out of my own head. Sometimes when I had nothing to do I sat in the patio and using my thumb and forefinger I would pull out whatever was causing me itching. I felt much relief on that spot afterwards.

●

Josefina has a new house on the other side of town and Carmen and I go to see the new house. My nieces, who I call cousins because they are around my age, show us the house and tell us their Dad is going to have it torn down and build a two-story house with a garden in the front in a year or so. I cannot believe the whole house will be torn down because it's a brick house and all the rooms have shiny smooth cement floors. It has a bathroom with a shower and toilet and it has a very small pool. The pool is square and about three feet high. It sits above the ground and it's made out of smooth cement. It's big enough for four people and I think it would be fun to fill it up with water and play in it.

At home we take baths in a giant pot, but the water in it is dirty and soapy so we cannot even sit in it. I am eight years old and have never played in clean water before and I hope I can play in this tiny pool before the house gets torn down. I like everything about this house, but I guess they want a house like the other rich people in the pueblo. I have never been inside a rich person's house, other than my sister's. But sometimes when I pass by one of those homes, the front door is open while the maid is mopping the living room and I can see white shiny tile floors, dark furniture pieces, and lush green plants in ceramic pots.

My sister's new house is very nice compared to our mud-brick house, but not compared to the homes of rich people. Our mud-brick house is better that the plain mud houses you see in the villages near the pueblo, so I feel some relief knowing that we do not live in one of the worst homes around. Our house was built when bricks were made out of mud and hay, but now only real bricks are being made. Most people living in villages, or ranchos as we call them, cannot afford real bricks so they make their homes themselves out of mud.

When I was little I used to scrape mud off one of the unpainted walls in the patio and eat it. It tasted very good and I wondered how they made mud-bricks that made them taste so good. The dirt in the back of the house, which we called the corral, was not as good so I only had it once. We poop in the back of the corral since we have no bathroom. So I made sure I had dirt near Ma's outdoor dirt oven, far away from the pooping area.

I am almost nine years old now and I'm glad I do not like to eat dirt anymore.

I stop thinking about rich people's houses and our own home when my sister tells us she has to run some errands and will be gone for a couple of hours. I do not like my sister and I'm glad she will be gone so I can play with my cousins. We play tag but get hot and tired quickly because it's the early afternoon and it is very warm. Carmen and I play tag all the time, but it is always at night when it is not hot anymore. We would like to fill up the small pool with water so we can play in it, but no one has any extra clothes for going in the water since they just got the house and it is practically empty.

Jaime, Josefina's son, has been in the house the whole time we have been here and even played tag with us. But now we wish he was not here so we could take off our clothes and go in the tiny pool. We beg him to go inside the house so we can go in the water. We do not want him to see us naked. He unhappily goes inside and we fill up the pool with water. My cousin Carmen and I have not had a bath in days and tell our cousins we should rinse off first so we will not get the pool water all dirty. We take off all of our clothes and rinse off together in their outdoor bathroom. The bathroom door was taken off for some reason and we are all under the shower when we see Jaime coming toward us smiling. We are completely naked and do not know what to do at first so we just stand there with Jaime staring at us. We finally run to the tiny pool. By this time we think it's kind of fun trying to keep Jaime from seeing our private parts so we do not ask him to go inside. My sister gets home and finds us naked in the pool and Jaime close to us trying to peek. She loses her temper and starts yelling at us. She tells us that Carmen and I are older than her daughters and should have known better. It's a sin to be naked in front of boys, so for sure Carmen and I are going to Hell because we are old enough to know it's a sin. We leave Josefina's house in shame and all I can think about is going to confession and telling the priest what I did so I will not go to Hell.

The following Saturday I cannot bring myself to go to confession. I do not want to go to Hell, but I am too ashamed to tell the priest what I did. Many Saturdays go by and I still cannot bring myself to go to confession. I feel so ashamed.

When I go to Mass on Sundays, I cannot have Communion and eat the bread. You can only have Communion and the bread if you go to confession the day before.

Over a year goes by before I go to confession. When I tell the priest my sin, he tells me kids do silly things like that and it is not a big sin. I have to say a Hail Mary every day for a week and I am very much forgiven.

•

The rainy season in the Pueblo usually starts in May and continues until August. Whenever it rains we have to be inside the house because it rains very hard and we have no umbrellas or raincoats. Besides, who wants to be outside when there is thunder and lightning that can kill you? Often after a rainstorm we hear of farmers being killed by lighting. The rains come fast and farmers do not have enough time to get back home. We only have electricity in our small living room and a couple other rooms. But the electricity usually goes out when it rains, so it does not matter which room you are in. Most of us kids prefer to be in Amelia's room because it has the fewest roof leaks. When the rain comes we have to get buckets and put them where we know the leaks are. There are always one or two leaks that have no buckets because we either run out of buckets or it's a leak that was not there before. After the buckets are full we have to empty them in the patio. The patio is in the center of the house with Lola's room and the kitchen on one side. Amelia's room, our tiny living room, and our own bedroom are in front.

Sometimes it starts to rain when we are eating supper and we have to run through the patio to get to Amelia's room. Our house is not very big, but by the time we get to Amelia's bedroom we are pretty wet. Every time my siblings, cousins, and I hear thunder and see lighting we feel scared. But Ma tells us we are not next to a tree so we'll be fine. We often get hail as well and it comes down so hard that it seems like the roof above us is going to collapse. The living room, which is between Amelia's room and our bedroom, opens up to the patio, so when it rains from a certain direction the floor gets very wet and slippery. This is also the room with the most leaks so we avoid it as much as possible. The rain usually lasts a few hours. When it stops raining our street gets flooded and we can go outside and play in the water. The water goes up to my knees most of the time and I have to hold my dress up. We have fun walking in the water and making paper boats. My sister Catalina says it is disgusting going in such dirty water. We do not care what she thinks. The water feels warm, it is sunny again, and the rainbow comes out. What could be better?

Every few years it rains much more than usual and the nearby river overflows. Our street gets so flooded that the water gets inside our house and we have to move to Josefina's house. Josefina tells Ma that's what we get for living at the edge of town so close to the river. And who was stupid enough to build a town so close to a river anyway?

I do not like to go in the water when the river overflows because the water in the river is black and oily. When it overflows you can still see the oil even though most of the water is fresh rain water.

Ma tells us the river used to be beautiful with clear, clean water, and lush green trees along the sides. All the women in the neighborhood used to wash their laundry there and my older brothers learned to swim there. But ever since the government built a petroleum refinery in Salamanca, the river has been black. Everyone in the pueblo complained when they saw what was happening to their river, but nothing was ever done. It is hard for me to imagine how the river looked when it was beautiful, since it looks so black and oily now. It smells bad and hardly anything grows along the sides.

•

The day long awaited by my cousins and sister-in-law is finally almost here. They will be leaving for El Norte in a few days. My sister, Teresa, will be buying a house soon and wants her kids to start having a better life as soon as possible. My sister-in-law Lola will also be leaving with her two sons, Toni, three years old, and Galo, just one.

As usual, bags do not have to be packed. They will leave all their belongings behind, except for a few things needed for the three-day bus trip to Tijuana. Teresa has arranged for someone to meet them in Tijuana and help them cross the border.

I feel content that my cousins are leaving since it is hard sharing a small room with so many people. I also feel that once my cousins leave maybe Ma will pay some attention to me. She always takes my cousin Irma shopping and gives extra attention to my cousin Carmen when she faints. We all know that Carmen fakes fainting when she does not get what she wants. But Ma puts a wet towel on her forehead anyway and has someone carry her to a bed. My other cousin, Miguel, with his light hair and piercing blue eyes, does not have to do much to get attention.

I feel kind of sad that my sister-in-law Lola is leaving. Other than my dad, she is the only person that is kind to me at home. She never calls me names and she lets me hold my nephews whenever I want to. She also lets me have some of their snacks, even though she does not get nearly as much money from her husband as my other sister-in-law, Amelia. I know I will miss my two little nephews, who are always giggly and loving.

I always knew this day would come, but now that it is here I feel jealous of my cousins. My cousins will be living in their own house with comfortable furniture, carpeted rooms, a bathroom, and a kitchen with a refrigerator stocked with their favorite foods. I know they will be getting new clothes and shoes and be able to go to school for as long as they wish. I have heard enough stories and seen enough pictures to be certain that this will happen, once they make it to El Norte.

What will I do when they come back to visit showing off all their new stuff like my cousin Helia did after being in El Norte for only a few months, I tell my best friend, Rosa Esperanza. You can spend a lot more time at my house so you won't have to be around them, she says to me.

On a warm sunny day – like most days in the Pueblo – my cousins and sister-in-law leave. They have no trouble crossing the border illegally, even though they have to walk for a while at night holding my two little nephews. After they leave, my three brothers finally have their own room. About a year later my sister-in-law, Amelia, also leaves with her two sons.

After Amelia leaves, my sister Catalina and I finally have our own bedroom, the best bedroom in the house. And since Amelia leaves everything behind, we have a comfortable bed, sheets, and a colorful warm bedspread. We also have our own dresser and all the soft bath towels we can possibly need.

When they are all gone the house seems empty. My brothers, who do not have to do any house chores, stay out most of the day. I do not like being home either, so after doing my chores and homework, I also leave our empty-feeling house.

●

Slowly I start to forget about El Norte. There are no more boxes of clothes arriving every other year. No more going to the post office with Ma to pick up a remittance from there. I think about the times when Ma took me to the post office to pick up a letter from the United States. The letters always had money orders inside and it was exciting waiting for Ma's name to be called.

The mail was called once a day and we had to stand in the small post office full of people. Most of the people there were peasants who lived outside the pueblo and when they opened their mouths, you could smell what they had just eaten. Since they had to walk or take a short bus trip to the pueblo, they usually ate something at the plaza before heading to the post office. Being tall for my age, I was not much shorter than most of them. I hated it when I was close to someone who had just eaten the sardines with lemon and chili sauce sold at one of the stands at the plaza.

Now when I walk through the plaza to my sister Josefina's house, I see some of these people waiting for the post office to open so they can pick up a remittance from El Norte. They are so lucky, I say to myself. We do not have anyone who sends us money anymore or the occasional toothbrushes, tooth pastes, or creamy soaps. And Ma does not go to the nearby city of Irapuato anymore to buy groceries. To go to Irapuato she needs much more than the small daily allowance Pa gives her.

•

After my cousins leave, I notice more people leaving for El Norte. The two single men living with their mom right next door suddenly leave. My sister's friend, a pretty girl with freckles and red hair, is also suddenly gone. She lived in our neighborhood and the whole pueblo knew her because one time she went to church kneeling the whole way to show her devotion to the church. It was not uncommon seeing women going to church on their knees as a sign of devotion, but most of these women were older. Teresa was barely sixteen or seventeen when she went to church on her knees. Some kids and grownups went along with her, putting old rugs on the rough concrete sidewalks to make it easier on her. She still got her knees all bloody.

Our play group gets smaller too. Two brothers who always played pretend games with my cousin Carmen, my best friend Esperanza, some other cousins, and I are also gone. When we pretended to be filming movies, they always played the husbands or boyfriends. Now they are gone, and no other boys want to play pretend games with us.

Our other neighbors, a family with three young women, also left. I will never forget them because the girls put ointments on my cousin and me when our arms and legs were covered with blisters from some kind of skin disease going around.

My brother Julian is sixteen years-old now and also wants to leave. Pa was able to afford paying for him to continue his education after he graduated from junior high school, but he now seems unable to continue paying. So Julian, unable to go to school or get a job in the pueblo, has no choice but to leave for El Norte like my other older brothers and sister.

I know I will not miss my brother. He is seven years older than I am and we hardly ever talk to each other. He sometimes makes comments about how chunky I was when I was a very little girl or how I have all the bad

Indian features. I never pay much attention to his rude comments. I have heard those comments many times before from other people.

After so many of my relatives leave the house for El Norte, my life gets easier. Ma does not beat me anymore and most of the time there is no one around to pick on me. We do not get money from the United States anymore, but a peaceful house makes up for that, most of the time.

With quite a few kids gone from our neighborhood, the street is also quieter. I do not like this much because we stop playing tag, hide-and-seek, and all the other fun games we used to play. For the first time I start playing alone, making little houses out of mud and using sticks for the dolls that live in them.

I keep loving school and do well in all my classes hoping that Pa will let me go to junior high after I finish sixth grade. My sister, Catalina, is actually going to junior high school, but Pa always complains about having to pay. Why does a girl need to go to school when all she is going to do is eventually get married and have babies? he always says. I know it will be harder for me to convince Pa to let me go to junior high than it was for my sister. Being one of the prettiest girls in the pueblo, she has a good chance of being able to work at our local bank or as a file clerk at one of the local government offices until she gets married.

●

I am finally used to our new lifestyle when one day Pa comes home with his face all swollen, a black eye, and bruises all over his body. I find out that while drunk he insulted a Federal and the cop got so mad he put Pa in jail and beat him. Now Pa needs to get away because he knows if that cop sees him again, he will put him in jail again, beat him, and maybe even kill him.

Pa leaves for El Norte as soon as he can. My brothers will pay for a coyote to smuggle him into the United States and they will help him get a job as a gardener. My brother Alfonso, being a hard worker, is now a supervisor for a sprinkler and landscaping company. So it will be fairly easy to get Pa a job.

I feel bad that Pa was beaten so badly, but in a way I am happy that he is leaving for the United States. I always thought that he would never go back there again. Ma, Catalina, and my brothers are happy as well. We know what it means to have someone in El Norte sending you money. And we cannot wait for the remittances to start coming.

I cannot help thinking about what we'll do with the money Pa will be sending us. With the money he sends maybe Ma can buy toilet paper, so I will not have to go through my old school papers looking for work I will not need any more to wipe with. Or maybe Ma can buy ham. I tasted ham once when the teachers at school had a meeting where they served ham sandwiches. They had a few left and gave them to some of the kids. I was lucky enough to get half of one and had enjoyed it so much.

After Pa leaves we talk about what will be the first thing we buy when the first money order arrives. We agree on tamales. We all like them and the ones from the lady that sells them on Sundays after church are especially good. We had them once in a while when Pa was here. The beef ones had meat without lots of fat.

We know we have to wait some time before the first remittance. Pa has to settle in, start working, save up enough money to send us, and then we have to wait for the slow Mexican mail service to deliver the remittance to our local post office.

We wait for weeks, then months, and nothing comes. Ma has been getting groceries on credit because the shop owner, Rafael, knows that Pa left for the United States. But after three months, he can no longer keep giving Ma credit.

He gives Ma a huge bag of lentil beans because he feels sorry for us and because he was happily married to Ma's sister for years until she passed away. We eat lentil beans every day for three weeks until finally the first letter with a money order in it arrives.

After cashing the money order Ma pays part of the money owed to Rafael and the next Sunday after church we get the tamales we have all been craving. The tamales are a big disappointment. My brother, Gerardo, finds a fly in one of them and I find a long black hair in one of mine. We stop eating them. That dirty lady must be making them surrounded by filth, Ma says.

My sister, Josefina, hears what happened to us and feeling sorry for us makes us tamales. As we are eating them we realize that she used pinto beans as the filling. They are the worst tamales we ever had.

●

After we received the first remittance, we think Pa will surely be sending them on a regular basis now. That does not happen. With the help of Josefina Ma keeps writing and calling my brothers in the United States to find out what is going on.

They tell Ma Pa is saving the money he is making so that when he goes back to the Pueblo he will have a lot of money. We have told him to send you money, but he will not listen. He is living with Manuel, not paying any rent, and has hardly any bills so he has plenty of money, they say.

Ma realizes it is hopeless to stay in the Pueblo. Pa will not be sending us money and there are no jobs any of us can get. She asks my brothers to send her money so she can go to El Norte.

●

As usual there are no bags to be packed. Ma and my sister just have to bring a change of clothes and some money for food along the way. The three-day bus trip will take them to Tijuana. There my brother Jose, who is now a legal resident, will find someone to help them cross the border.

Ma and my sister, along with a large group of mostly Mexicans, cross the border with the help of a coyote on their first attempt. Ma, who is in her early fifties, finds the crossing very difficult. The group has to run over rocky hills at night for many hours. My sister Catalina, who is sixteen years old, does not find the ordeal as difficult. The group, composed mostly of men, goes out of their way to help my very pretty sister. Worried about my sister's safety, Ma tries to keep up with the young group, but it is of no use. She stays behind the group the whole way, barely able to stay close enough to see them.

•

My two brothers and I stay with Josefina. None of us like her and we do not want to stay with her even though she is married to a rich man and her house is much better than ours. It has a big bathroom, a big dining room, and all the rooms have shiny smooth cement floors. Compared to most of the homes in the pueblo, this is a very good house. Nonetheless, they are still planning on having it torn down and building a two-story house in its place.

Ma told us we only had to stay with Josefina for a few months. Once she made it to El Norte she would make Pa give her all the money he has been saving, maybe make some money herself, and then come back.

To my brothers and me, a few months seemed like an eternity.

•

It's only our second day in Josefina's house and she is already yelling at us. She is yelling at my brother Gerardo because yesterday he did not come home for supper and because he stayed out late. She is yelling at my brother Enrique and me because yesterday we did not help her enough around the house. Concha and Chayo (her daughter's nicknames) did not do any work, we blurt out. They were busy all day, she yells back.

The next few days she keeps giving my brothers chores. Gerardo refuses to do them and stays out all day. Enrique, who never did any chores back at home, attempts to do them, but does such a bad job sweeping the floors that I end up doing the work.

Things go from bad to worse when one day she takes off with her daughters and tells me I need to clean the whole house and wash all the dishes by the time they get back. By the time I am finished sweeping and mopping the floors and cleaning the kitchen, I am exhausted. I am used to doing chores, unlike my brothers who never did any chores in the house because Pa said house chores were only for women. But I never had to clean a whole house before. I decide it is only fair to leave the dishes for Concha and Chayo, so I stack the many dishes, pots, pans, cups, glasses and utensils in a great big pile on the floor. When my sister gets back, she is so upset that I did not do the dishes that she kicks the pile. The dishes land all over the floor and I end up having to pick them up and wash them.

After almost two weeks my brothers and I have had enough. We leave her house and go back to our empty house on the other side of the Pueblo. We can live on our own, the three of us agree. Gerardo says, I am already thirteen and I can work in the fields and support the two of you. I will take care of the house, I say, and go to school when it starts. Enrique will just go to school, we decide.

Gerardo gets some work at a wheat field and brings home some money. It's only enough for a meal, but we are happy that we are not with our sister. I make beans and even have money for some white cheese to sprinkle over the boiled beans. We are determined to live in our house until Ma gets back, even if we eat just beans every day.

Our Aunt Victoria, Ma's sister-in-law who lives nearby, brings us some food when she hears that we are home alone. We tell her Josefina made us do chores all day, while she and her daughters did not do any.

Niños (children), she says, you don't have go back to her house. I'll bring you food every day until your ma comes back. I know Josefina and how difficult she can be. You do not have to live with her.

For days we are happy living on our own. Gerardo is making money by spreading seeds on a farm field. I am taking care of the house and cooking and Enrique, who is only nine, spends the whole day playing outside. Our fun ends when on the fourth day Josefina comes to get us. We do not want to go back to her house, but we know we do not have a choice.

When we get to her house her husband is there and he tells her to stop yelling at us. She says she won't have to much longer because she called Ma and told her all the trouble we are causing. Ma said not to enroll us in school again because she is going to send us money so we can join her and the rest of the family in El Norte.

My whole body becomes numb from emotion when I hear this. I have never in my life felt so happy, lucky, fortunate, and hopeful.

The next day Josefina tells me I have to go to our school and tell them we will not be enrolling for the coming school year. As I am walking to the school, I feel like yelling that I am going to El Norte to everyone I pass by. I am quite shy so I do not. It is almost September so there is a lady behind a small, old, light green desk at the entrance of the school talking to a couple of parents. When she is finished with them, I tell her my two brothers and I are not coming back to school in September. We are leaving for El Norte in a couple of weeks. She tells me she is happy for me.

As I am walking to my best friend's house to tell her the good news, I think about how relieved I am that I will not be in the sixth grade class. My brother, Gerardo, who is two years older than I am, would have been in the same class because he failed to pass sixth grade again. Being in the same class as my brother would have been bad, but even worse than that was the sixth grade teacher. This teacher had the reputation of being the meanest teacher in the school. If you did not do your homework or behave she would hit you hard. If you were not very proficient in all the subjects she taught, she would not let you pass sixth grade. I always did my homework and behaved in class, but I was afraid of failing her class. I never had to repeat a grade, but I had heard that sixth grade was very tough to pass. This was the last grade in elementary school, the last year in school for most kids in the Pueblo. To pass this grade you had to know geometry and be very good at writing. I had always liked math – it made so much sense – but did not care for geometry when it was introduced in fifth grade. Thank God I will be going to El Norte and will not have to worry about all this, I say to myself.

I get to my friend's house and tell her the good news. When I come back to visit, I will bring you new clothes and I promise I will not act conceited, I tell her. She tells me she has a brother living in El Norte and she has only seen him once since he left. Her other brother will probably be leaving soon and maybe I will see them up there.

I then go to my Aunt Candelaria's house. She lives just a few houses away from my friend's house. She is Ma's sister, the only sister alive. She is very short and chunky – unlike Ma – and has pretty hazel eyes. I like her because she is always kind to us and because whenever we felt sick, she would come to see us and tell Ma what she could do to help us get better. She knows all of the different herbs and how they should be used to cure people. I have never seen a doctor in my life and she is the closest thing to a doctor that I know. She tells me she is happy for my brothers and me. She misses her sister, but knows that leaving for El Norte was the best thing Ma could have done. I wish I had been able to help her when she was here, she says, but we barely have enough money to feed ourselves. And you know it is impossible for women our age to find any type of work in this poor town. So your Ma had no choice.

I knew she wanted to help Ma and even gave her a little money when we most needed it. But her husband, Salvador, who did kind of the same work as Pa, barely made enough money for themselves. Unlike Pa, who bought cattle and then sold them to our local meat markets for a good profit, Salvador bought and sold pigs and chickens for a small profit. Tia (Aunt) Candelaria, also had a son in El Norte, but he was not sending them much money. So she had to work all day helping her husband with the pigs and chickens.

Do not forget about us when you make it in El Norte, she says. I feel so proud when I hear her say this because she said when, not if.

My cousin Juana tells me she wishes she could go to El Norte as well. But who would hire me with this disabled arm of mine? she says.

81

When we were little Ma told us what happened to my Tia's third-oldest daughter. When Juana was a baby, Tia Candelaria was working in the hot sun and trying to nurse her at the same time. Baby Juana had a convulsion and was never the same again. Now she walks around town limping and unable to use one of her arms. She makes money working as a maid for the rich people in our town.

Anyway, Juana says, I heard that in El Norte you cannot walk all over the place. If you are not working, you just sit around in your house and you have to drive or be driven everywhere you go. I do not think I would like that.

They wish me good luck and say to be sure to visit them when I come back. I then go to my Tia Victoria's house. She is short and chunky too – like almost all older women in the Pueblo. Tia Victoria also has a son in El Norte. Pedro, the oldest, whose big family lives with Tia, has been in El Norte as long as my brothers. Her other son, Juan, will probably be leaving soon. He is the only one in the family who has gone to our local junior high school. My Tia is very proud of him for that, but even with a higher education than most people in the pueblo, it is practically impossible for him to find a job. So it will just be a matter of time before he heads for Los Angeles and joins his brother. Los Angeles is where most people that head for El Norte end up. Tia Victoria also has a son in Mexico City. Her son is very glad he went to Mexico City instead of El Norte because he has a good-paying job working in a plastics factory.

I thank her for helping us when we were home alone and she wishes me good luck. Be sure you tell Pedro that I am doing just fine, she says. My cousin, Pedro's daughter Helia, who is about my age, tells me she hopes I like El Norte. She was there for quite a few months and did not like it because she could not go anywhere. She was making some money babysitting my brother's kids and would have gone to school if she had stayed longer. I always thought she was crazy for coming back because she could not walk anywhere, but never told her because I did not want to get in a fight with her. I always felt that if I ever made it to El Norte, I would have to be dragged by my feet out of such a wonderful country and back into Mexico.

I still feel that way and say to Helia, I do not think I will be coming back for a long time. I will miss my Tias and the delicious whole wheat biscuits my Tia Victoria makes during the wheat harvest season, but going to El Norte is what I have been dreaming about for years.

•

For the next week and a half all I think about is going to El Norte. I have heard so many good things about it, but even so I simply cannot picture it. When my brothers used to come, they always talked about the gigantic grocery stores they went to every week to shop for food. They also talked about how clean everything was and the fact that there were no flies inside the homes. We had so many flies in our tiny kitchen back in our house that we did not even try to kill them. What was the use? The kitchen, which was right next to our open patio, did not have a door and if we killed the flies, more would just keep coming. There are even flies at my sister's house and on the street. I do not think I have ever been in a house that does not have any flies.

Waiting for the day when we finally leave for El Norte is agonizing. There is nothing to do but wait. There is nothing to pack and I have already said good-bye to my friends and relatives.

Living with Josefina is easier now. She is not yelling at us as much and does not give us as many chores. Ever since Ma called and told Josefina her decision to send for us, Josefina's attitude toward us changed.

One of the reasons why I was always jealous of my cousins, Irma, Carmen, and Miguel, was because most people treated them better than other kids in the neighborhood. And I knew that the reason why they did this was because everyone knew that sooner or later they would leave for El Norte. Kids that left for El Norte had the opportunity to make something of themselves and come back to the Pueblo educated and with money.

I am enjoying the better treatment from Josefina. Although they have money, they are not among the richest families in the pueblo. There are a few families with a lot more land, tractors, and trucks. I think she is treating us better because she feels that maybe someday she might need our help, I say to my brothers. They both agree.

Her husband, who is one of those rare people that treats everyone with respect, does not treat us any differently. But I know that instead of feeling sorry for us, he now feels hopeful for us. I sometimes cannot believe how he treats us so much better than our own sister. Please listen to your sister so she will not get mad and yell at you, he sometimes says to us.

I often feel my sister does not deserve this man. With his blue eyes, white skin, happy demeanor, and money he could have had any woman he wanted. Why my sister? I will miss listening to his stories about trips he takes. He is one of the few men in the pueblo that has a car, so when he is not supervising his farm he travels alone for business and with his family for fun. Ma liked him a lot too, but often said that he exaggerated too much when he talked about his travels.

My sister's kids, Jaime, Concha, and Chayo, who I call cousins because they are about my age, have always been friendly to my brothers and me. Their attitude toward us does not change when they hear we will be living for El Norte.

I was always glad they were like their dad and not like my sister. Like their father they never put us down for wearing dirty, wrinkled clothes, which was something my sister often did. They did keep their friendships separate, inviting us to play in their house

85

only when their rich friends were not around and never inviting us along when they went to play at one of their friend's house. But I never blamed them for this. We all knew that rich kids did not play with lower class kids.

●

I know I will kind of miss them. Jaime, with his blond hair and blue eyes, looks so much like his dad. He has a happy demeanor like his dad too. And just like his dad, he loves telling stories. After coming back from every vacation, he would visit us and tell us where they went and what they did. Ma would just nod her head and smile. After he left she would say, that boy exaggerates just like his father, but they sure are entertaining.

When I used to visit my sister, I sometimes felt sorry for Jaime. My sister usually gave him more chores than her daughters and beat him with a belt if he did not do them. He was the oldest, but he had to do chores like wash dishes and sweep and mop floors, chores that are not done by men in the pueblo. Besides, his sisters were old enough to do those chores.

My cousin Concha – everyone calls her by her nickname – whose real name is Leticia, also has blond hair, blue eyes, and white skin. She is my favorite cousin. I play with her more than with any other relative. And whenever she visited us, she always brought money to buy a snack. If it were not for her, I would not have known what potato chips, Twinkies, and cupcakes tasted like. My fifty centavos weekly allowance was never enough to buy any of these expensive treats. I will miss her the most.

My other cousin, Chayo, the youngest of the three, has brown hair, brown eyes, and light skin. She is three years younger than I am so I never really play with her. She is only eight years old, but she knows what the rich people in the pueblo are up to and likes to tell us. She once told us, Papa and his friends are going to build a hall for meetings and parties, but only members of the club we belong to will be able to use it. I really do not care what the rich people in our town are up to, but I do not want to be rude to Chayo. So I just smile and pretend I am happy for them. I will miss Chayo the least.

●

The day of our departure finally arrives. We wear our best clothes and head for the plaza to take the bus that will take us to Irapuato. As we are walking to the plaza with our sister Josefina, I am hoping to run into people I know so I can tell them we are leaving for El Norte. But I do not see anyone I know. I recognize most people we pass – after all, everyone in the Pueblo recognizes each other – but I do not know their names. An older lady wearing a dark dress way below her knees is sweeping the front of her house and asks my sister if we are leaving the Pueblo. My sister tells her we are and the lady wishes us good luck. I am glad at least someone knows we are leaving.

My brothers and I wish Josefina was not going with us. None of us like her. She has never said a kind thing to any of us and we cannot wait to be away from her. But Ma asked her to take us all the way to Tijuana, so we will have to ride in buses with her for three days until we get there. We hope that once we make it to Tijuana that we will not see her for a very long time.

We board the first bus at the plaza and we have to wait until it fills up. It is just past twelve. I know this because the church with the loud bell is right next to the plaza and it rang twelve just a little while ago. As I sit on the rusty metal seats with blue paint peeling all over, I wonder if I will ever hear our church bell again.

The church bell runs our daily schedules since most people in the pueblo do not have clocks in their homes or wear watches. The bell gives us the time, informs us that Mass will be starting soon, and lets us know when there is a wedding, a Baptism, or a funeral in the pueblo.

The bus is supposed to leave at twelve, but it will not leave until most of the seats are taken. So I sit there and look at the people getting in. Most of them are peasant-looking – dark skin with Indian features – and dress worse than most of the people who live in the pueblo, so I figure they must be from nearby villages. We call these villages, ranchos.

It amazes me how ranchos can be so different from the Pueblo. Most of them have six to ten mud houses, with no electricity or running water. The few times that I went to Irapuato with Ma, I would always see dirty toddlers running around with no underwear as we passed by some of these villages. It was peculiar to see how everyone in the ranchos seemed to look alike, either very dark or very light, unlike the Pueblo where you saw all kinds of people, dark, light, and white. It is well known that the ranchos with light people became that way because when the Spanish came the women living there were attacked. Since these ranchos were far away from each other their children could not mix with Indians from other ranchos.

I have heard of ranchos where rich land owners live, but I have never seen one. Buses do not go by them since most people living there have trucks for transportation. These ranchos have big brick houses, I have been told, and the people living there own the land nearby. Most of these people are white with blue eyes and when they come to the Pueblo in their trucks, you see them wearing cowboy hats and pointy boots.

The bus is finally full and it takes off. I never thought I would feel sad when I left the Pueblo – *Pueblonuevo* – it is called, but I actually do. All I ever wanted to do since I can remember was to leave for El Norte, but now that I am going it makes me sad to leave behind all I have ever known. As we ride by in the bus, I look at the colorful houses – green, blue, red, orange – right next to each other and with paint peeling all over. I see the small colorful wood doors of many of these houses. Our house has a small door too and I think about how Pa had to bend his head going in and out of our house.

I see the lack of windows and gardens on most houses. When I pass a house with windows and a garden in the front, I know it belongs to either one of our local doctors – we have two of them – or a rich land owner. I look at the people outside, walking to a nearby store or to the plaza or just standing in front of their houses gossiping with their neighbors. And I see kids wearing dirty, wrinkled clothes, playing outside their homes.

It takes just a short time to reach the outskirts of the pueblo. Now there are only wheat and corn fields and cows grazing here and there. We pass men riding on bicycles – just like Pa did sometimes when he had to go from rancho to rancho to buy cattle – and trucks pass us driven by farmland owners. I am not sad anymore and cannot wait to get to Irapuato, where we will be taking a second bus to Guadalajara. The bus makes a couple of stops and lets off some peasant-looking men wearing sombreros and carrying boxes tied with ropes. I look at them and feel sorry for them because they have to walk for a while before they get to their village and they are wearing old dress shoes, long sleeve shirts, and long pants on this hot September day.

It has been almost an hour since we left El Pueblo and I know we are getting close to Irapuato because I start seeing less farm land and start seeing trash along the road. People are not supposed to throw their trash along the outskirts of their city or town, but they do it anyway. There is also rusty, useless farm equipment on land not being used for any purpose. We reach the cracked, paved streets of Irapuato, where there are lots of small old cars parked on the street or being driven by hurried drivers. The cars are noisy and have dark fumes coming out of them. I think about how happy I was when Ma brought me here a few times to do some shopping, but now I miss the peacefulness of the Pueblo with its cobblestone streets and no noisy cars.

The closer we get to the bus terminal the more people we see selling oranges and peanuts in the middle of the streets. There are people everywhere, carrying bags, carrying baskets on top of their heads, or just walking hurriedly. My sister wants to take the two o'clock bus to Guadalajara, so we have to hurry and get tickets.

We get the tickets on time and board the bus. This bus is much more comfortable than the old rusty, noisy bus we took in the Pueblo. My butt still hurts from sitting on the metal seat and bouncing up and down over our cobblestone streets and the dirt roads for over an hour. I am sure my brother, Gerardo, is in pain as well, since we are both very skinny and have flat butts.

The bus takes off shortly after two and I am thankful for the cushiony seats and the relatively smooth paved road to Guadalajara. I am sitting next to my sister,

Josefina, and I have nothing to say to her. All I ever heard from her was screaming, so I do not know how to have a conversation with her. The bus does not make stops like the bus from the Pueblo and I assume they must have other buses that take people to their ranchos from Irapuato. The bus takes four hours to get to Guadalajara, but I do not mind because the seats are so soft and cushiony.

We arrive in Guadalajara in the late afternoon. The bus terminal there is like the one in Irapuato, full of people and vendors selling peanuts, oranges, tortas (Mexican sandwiches), toys, and other stuff. We do not have to catch the bus that will take us to Tijuana until nighttime, so we have time to walk around the terminal and have some dinner. We have tortas with Mexican cheese in them for dinner. My brothers and I wanted tortas with ham in them, but Josefina told us she had to buy us food for three days and she could not be wasting the money on ham tortas. It is fun walking around the terminal without Josefina and I wish Ma had not sent all the money for this trip to her. There are so many things to buy and we do not have a cent in our pocket. There is a big clock at the terminal so we know when it's time to go where all the buses are and look for Josefina.

We board an even newer bus than the one we took from Irapuato. It has gray padded seats and windows without any scratches. I have never seen such a new and clean bus and I do not think it will be bad spending three days riding it. Josefina lets me have the window seat, but it is night now so I cannot see much when I look outside. The bus leaves Guadalajara and I wonder if I will ever be able to come back here, for I like this city much more than Irapuato. When we arrived in Guadalajara, I did not see as many old cars with dark smoke coming out of them as in Irapuato. And when the bus went by some big churches, I had felt like getting out of the bus and going inside them. They were so much bigger that the churches in the Pueblo and I felt certain they were also prettier inside.

Sitting comfortably in the bus I think about my favorite church back home, the one with the big bell. This was the church reserved for weddings, Communions and Baptisms. The church made out of gray stones was used for Masses. Whenever I was in my favorite church, I would spend the whole time looking at the angels painted on the ceiling, the walls with colorful paintings and gold trim, and the saints who wore beautiful satin pastel dresses, capes, and gold crowns. All the saints had creamy white skin, big eyes, pointy noses, and small lips.

I often wondered if there were any saints that looked like me. I had heard that the Virgin of Guadalupe looked more Indian. But when I saw I picture of her, I did not think she had small eyes, a chunky nose, and full lips like me. I will miss our church and our friendly priests even though I, like everyone else in the Pueblo, had to kiss one of their hands every time we saw them. But I will not miss people thinking that only girls who look somewhat like our virgins are pretty.

I always noticed how men stared at girls with pointy noses and small mouths, and also at women with small waists, big hips, and legs that were not skinny. I do not have a pointy nose or small mouth. I am only eleven, but I am so tall and skinny I cannot imagine ever having big hips. My legs are long and skinny too and I now feel thankful that we left the Pueblo because I just remembered all the times that I felt afraid I would not be able to find a husband when I got older.

My sister gives me a blanket and I fall asleep. When I wake up the next morning my body is all sore. We are in a different city now, but I do not care which city it is since I have been in buses now for almost a full day and I feel tired. Today and tomorrow we will be making stops in different cities, but they are all starting to look the same and I just want to get to Tijuana so we can cross the border into El Norte.

●

We arrive at Tijuana's bus terminal with sore bodies and hungry. My oldest brother, Jose, is supposed to be waiting for us inside the terminal with his American-citizen wife. I do not think my brothers or I will recognize Jose since we have not seen him in over five years. He was home for a few days once after being deported and sent way south into Mexico.

The bus terminal is big and crowded but Josefina manages to spot my brother. He looks very different from how I remembered him. He is not as skinny and does not look as tall as before. He comes over to us with a friendly smile and greets us. He introduces us to his wife, a nice looking older woman with very light skin and blond hair. My sister, Josefina, is pleasant and all smiles at them. I wonder how she can be so nice to some people, but so mean to us. I know the trip was tough, my brother says, but hopefully soon you will be able to see Ma and everyone else. Tonight we will stay in a hotel and tomorrow you will try to cross the border. We found a couple that will take you in their car across the border as their children. You are very lucky because everyone, including Ma, Alfonso's and Manuel's toddlers had to cross through the hills.

Thank you for bringing them all the way to Tijuana, he says to my sister. I wish you would stay with us tonight and get a good night's sleep. That would be nice, Josefina says, but I have to get back to my children. For the second time in my life, I feel Josefina has done something commendable. Six straight days riding in a bus is no easy task.

My brother takes us to a restaurant to get some dinner. I have never been to a restaurant before and I feel my life has already started to change. Tijuana reminds me of Irapuato, crowded and noisy. Back at the hotel my brother says to us, it should be easy for you to cross the border. All you need to do is learn a few

English words and pretend the couple you will be with are your parents. The words you need to learn are yes, okay, and my name is... You also need to learn where you are supposed to live and where you were born. Alicia will help you learn all that. Tomorrow, we will take you shopping for new clothes so you will look like you are from El Norte and you will meet the couple. I have only gone shopping for clothes once in my life, so I cannot wait until the next day.

It is Sunday morning and all the stores are crowded. Jose takes my brothers and I go with his wife. What kind of outfit would you like? Alicia asks me. I would really like to get pants, I answer. I had a pair of pants a couple of years ago and I really liked them. I am tall and skinny and it is hard finding pants that fit me. I finally find something that fits me. An orangey pantsuit with bell bottoms; it is the best outfit I have ever put on. I leave it on and Alicia throws away my old clothes.

I am not even in El Norte yet and I am already so happy. I got a new outfit, my brother buys us whatever we want to eat, and no one has yelled at us since we got here.

It's Sunday afternoon, the busiest time at the San Ysidro checkpoint, and we meet the couple that is going to help us cross the border. They are both Mexican and very friendly. Practice what you learned before you get to the checkpoint, my brother says to us. My brothers and I practice saying our names in English and try to stay calm.

There are many cars in front of us waiting to get through and the line moves very slowly. When we get near the front, a tall American in a greenish uniform and dark hat comes by, looks in the car, and asks us if the people in the front are our parents. We calmly say yes and he waves us off. With a huge sense of relief, we drive away from the check point.

It is starting to get dark and I cannot see much more than the smooth, lighted, wide road we are on. We get off the road, which the man driving called the freeway, and head to a store where we are supposed to meet my brother and his wife again.

I always expected El Norte to be beautiful, but what I am seeing is beyond all my expectations. Big trees and palm trees are everywhere on well-lit, clean streets. The cars on the street are clean and do not emit smoke or make loud rumbling noises like the ones in Irapuato or Tijuana. There are tall buildings with no paint peeling off and with colorful flowers in the front. No wonder my brothers came back here as soon as possible after being deported.

We wait in the car for my brother in front of the biggest store I have ever seen. We do not have to wait long before we spot my brother's car. He sees our car as well and parks close by. Our job is done, say the couple. Your brother will take you the rest of the way. We are glad we were able to reunite you kids with your parents. Jose and his wife smile at us as soon as they see us. They shake hands with the man and lady that my brothers and I are so thankful for. After a few minutes of conversation among the adults, we wave at the couple and they drive off. Are you hungry? Jose asks us. We are starving since it has been a few hours since we ate. We shyly say yes since we are not accustomed to having someone do so much for us.

We go inside the grocery store and Jose gives us ten dollars each to buy any kind of snack we want. He knows what a shock it is for us to be in such a big grocery store with so much food, so he takes us around the different aisles showing us things we can buy. The store is bright and the floors are so clean and shiny I wish we could stay here for hours, but Ma and the rest of the family are waiting for us so we cannot take our time looking at everything we pass by. We go by the cold meats section and I just have to know what the price of ham is. One dollar and thirty-nine cents is the price for a good size package of ham. I just cannot believe my eyes. Ma was never able to buy ham for us back in the Pueblo and here I am able to buy some and have plenty of money left over. We end up buying a huge bag of chips and bean dip, which Jose says will go well with the chips, and some soft drinks. He pays for everything and tells us to keep our money. The most money I ever had was a dollar and having ten dollars makes me feel rich.

As we eat our chips and bean dip in the car I continue to be amazed by all the trees, buildings, and lights we see from the car. After a few hours of driving, we get off the freeway and Jose says we are very close to

Teresa's house. We will be staying with her. Ma and Pa are staying with Manuel in a guest house right behind Teresa's house and they are all up waiting for us. I wonder if Teresa's house looks like the houses we are passing by, each one with grass and trees in the front. The only grass we saw in the Pueblo was in the plazas – the regular plaza with the kiosk and the one called the "Jardin" (garden).

We drive into Teresa's house, a house much bigger than any we have seen so far. It's quite dark, but I can see the house with a big lawn in the front on one side and on the other side what seems to be a vegetable garden. We drive in on a long dirt driveway which is right in the center.

When the car stops I see Ma and Pa come out of the house, Ma is not as skinny and Pa is much heavier than I remembered him. We go in through the kitchen and I want to stop and look at all the appliances and furniture, but Ma says everyone is in the living room so I barely have a chance to take a look. The living room is bright and warm and everyone stands up when they see us.

All the women are wearing long robes and I wonder if soon I will be getting a long robe to wear at night too. It has only been two years since my cousins left the Pueblo, but it feels like ten when I talk to them. Irma has long shiny hair and clear skin. Carmen has short hair as she always did and she also has clear skin.

Irma tells me I will probably be going to the same school she does. There are only a few Mexicans in the school, but lately more are starting to come. She is finished taking E.S.L. (English as a Second Language) classes, but knows the teacher and some of the people still taking these classes so she will introduce me to them. She is in ninth grade now. It will be her last year at the school and then she will be going to high school. I am very glad to hear I will be in junior high since I was going into sixth grade in Mexico and did not really think I would be able to go to junior high. Besides I am so tall, even though I am only eleven years old, no one will think I am skipping a grade.

My cousin Carmen is in sixth grade even though she is almost a year older than I am. She tells me all her friends are American because there are no Mexicans in her school. Her brother Miguel learned English right away and is now the best player on his Little League team.

My sister Teresa reminds me of Josefina, short and kind of heavy, but with much darker skin and some Indian features. She did not seem very happy to see us and I wonder why, since she knows of our suffering in the Pueblo. My brother Manuel looks about the same, tall and skinny, and he does not seem happy to see us either. He nods his head and says "hey" to us when we approach him. His wife, Lola, is also skinny even though she had another baby just a few months ago. She smiles at us and tells us we can see little Tony, Galo, and the new baby girl tomorrow. My brother Julian is staying in Teresa's house too, but Ma did not wake him up when we arrived because he is so busy all the time, working all day and going to night school right after work. Ma tells us he only has time to take a shower and eat dinner after work. After school he goes straight to bed.

It is late so everyone has to go to bed. Ma asks us if we are hungry and we tell her we are not. We ate tons of chips and bean dip, but some milk would be good. She goes into the kitchen and before I follow her, I stand and admire everything around me. The huge, comfortable green couch, the soft clean carpet underneath my feet, the big windows with pretty see-through curtains, the big television, and the tables placed just right on each side of the couch. No wonder my brothers hated being deported to Mexico. All we had in our living room, if you can call it that, were a couple of green wood chairs with paint peeling off. It was the room with the best floor, cold, dark green shiny cement with some cracks in it. I had always liked our living room floor for it was much nicer than the rough cement in our patio or the dirt floors of two of the bedrooms.

Once in the kitchen, Ma hands us each a tall glass of cold milk. My brothers and I look at each other. We have never had so much milk before. How can they have so much of everything here? we ask Ma. This is a rich country, she says. In the Pueblo, all we got was a little cup of warm milk in the morning. It was warm because

Ma had to boil it first and it was gone before it had a chance to completely cool off.

When Pa brought a cow home before selling it to the butcher at the meat market, we often milked it and took sips of the warm milk before handing the container over to Ma. I like this cold milk better. It is so refreshing and I wonder if there is anything I will not like better than in Mexico.

Looking at Teresa's kitchen I realize everything will be better here. The kitchen has a big stove and refrigerator, a new-looking round table with comfortable chairs, and it has two sinks. Back at home we had to wash the dishes on the ground in the patio using buckets for washing and rinsing. The table we ate on was small and the wood chairs we sat on were hard and uncomfortable. Our gas stove was half the size of this one and Ma could not use it a lot because the gas tank attached to it could only be replaced when the truck selling gas tanks drove by on our street. Besides, even if the truck came by more often, we probably would not have money to replace the tank.

As impressive as everything is, nothing seems more impressive than the gigantic refrigerator stocked with all kinds of food. When times were good in the Pueblo, Ma got twenty pesos a day for groceries and that was barely enough for our two meals a day and Mexican bread at night. I am sure Ma would have liked to have a refrigerator, but what would be the use? She only got enough money to make the food we would be eating that day and nothing left over to store.

After our milk Ma hands us sleeping clothes. We almost always slept in the clothes we were wearing back home, so we do not know where to change or what to do with the clothes she hands us. She tell us we can change in the bathroom and that tomorrow we will be getting toothbrushes so we can brush our teeth before going to bed. She also tells us we will have to take a bath tomorrow. People here take baths every day, not once a week like in Mexico.

I am finally in bed with one of my cousins, but I cannot fall asleep. I keep thinking about the gigantic grocery store with the packages of ham for one dollar and thirty-nine cents. I wanted to buy it, but my brother Jose said it would be hard to make ham sandwiches in the car. Besides, he said, you are in El Norte now, you can have ham sandwiches every day if you want to. I had had a craving for ham for years, ever since one of my teachers gave us leftover sandwiches from a meeting, but it was the most expensive meat at the meat shop and Ma could never afford it. Now I could have it every day if I wanted to. How unreal.

As I lie in bed with my cousin, Irma, I start to worry. What about immigration? My brothers were deported often. Most of the time they were deported to Tijuana and they sneaked right back, but I am only eleven and I would not be able to come right back. What does immigration look like? Do they drive by in the streets and how often? My cousins do not seem worried about it. I probably do not have to worry about it either. I hope.

I start falling asleep listening to cars driving by, not noisy cars like the ones in Mexico, but fast moving, smooth sounding cars. Before falling asleep, I feel all kinds of emotions come over me. I feel *peace, joy, and enormous opportunity. I am in America now. Everything will be okay.*

Alfonso, before he left Mexico for the first time.

Jose, in the late 1960's a couple of years after arriving in the U.S.

Alfonso, his wife Amelia, and their son Armando vacationing in Mexico.

Enrique's first picture in the U.S., he was nine years old.

Gerardo in the U.S., pictured here at age twenty.

Third Grade class picture, author is in the center of the second row from the top.

Recent picture of Santos Degollado Elementary School, the school has not changed much.

Fourth Grade class picture, author is fourth from the left in the top row. Author's best friend, Rosa Esperanza, is right next to the teacher. Most of the kids in this picture immigrated to the United States at some point in their lives.

The author in seventh grade with the E.S.L. teacher's aide at Sutter Jr. High.

The Pueblo's Saint,
Santa Candelaria

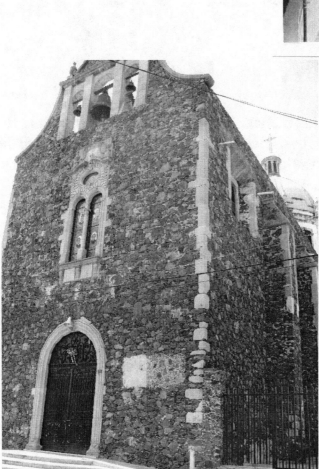

The stone church, called "El Templo".

Recent picture of the church used for weddings, Baptisms, and Communions. It is called "La Parroquia".

Recent picture of the Parroquia, Santa Candelaria is in the front center and up high protected by glass.

Adored religious statue in the state of Guanajuato. This mountain top statue is called "Cristo Rey" and it is visited by hundreds of thousands of people each year.

The statue of Cristo Rey is visible from many miles away.

Recent photo of the main plaza in Pueblonuevo.

Recent photo of a farm and home surrounding Pueblonuevo.

Recent photo of the front of the author's former house.

Author's High School Senior Picture

Part Two

Hope and Opportunity

I wake up the next day feeling a little like a new person. I know my life will be completely different now and thinking about it makes my body feel warm all over. My cousins Irma and Carmen have left for school already. Early this morning I heard a loud sound – which turned out to be an alarm clock – and Irma got up to turn it off. She then put on clothes that were neatly laid out on a table. Carmen got up a few minutes later, but I don't know which clothes she put on since I went right back to sleep. I cannot wait to start school, but I am glad that I probably won't be going for a couple more days. Everything is so different and I want to try my best at adjusting.

My cousin's room is much lighter now than when I first woke up this morning. Now I can see how pretty it is. Carmen's bed has been neatly made and I can see Irma's bed has a colorful matching bedspread. There is a small table with a small lamp on top of it and everything in the room seems to be in its place. The sheer curtains are letting the morning sun rays in all the way down to the carpet. I think the carpet looks funny; it is light brown and it almost looks like the coat of a hairy animal.

Ma comes into the room and gives me some clothes to put on. She tells me she gave me shorts to put on because it is going to be a hot day. After she leaves the room, I put on the shorts and top. I have never worn shorts before and I do not like them because they make my legs look so long and skinny. I am glad I never had to wear shorts like this in Mexico because people would have laughed at me since there they like legs with meat on them, not bony legs like mine. I make Irma's bed the same way Carmen made hers and look around the room again, amazed at how pretty it looks.

I go over to Lola's house which is right behind Teresa's house. It looks much older than Teresa's house. The kitchen is the first room I see when I open the door and I see Ma and Lola cooking breakfast. Pa and my two older brothers, Manuel and Julian, have left for work already. Everyone else is still sleeping. Lola is wearing shorts like I am. She has skinny legs too so I start feeling a little more comfortable wearing shorts. Lola is still very friendly and does not seem to have changed nearly as much as my cousins.

A couple of hours later I meet Lola's newest child. Her name is Connie, which is the English translation of Ma's name, Consuelo, I am told. She has shiny curly black hair, big brown eyes, chunky cheeks, and is the prettiest baby I have ever seen. Lola tells me she was born with a head full of shiny curly back hair. The nurses in the hospital all wanted to hold her because she was such a pretty baby and they rarely saw a baby being born with a head full of shiny black hair. Connie is the first baby in our family to be born in El Norte. I think about how lucky she is to be born in such a wonderful country. I also meet my nephews, Tony and Galo. They are happy little kids just like they were in Mexico.

Later in the day Ma shows me how to take a bath in Teresa's bathroom. So far I have liked everything about

Teresa's house, but I think I like this warm bath most of all. I never knew how enjoyable a bath could be.

After a couple of nights of sleeping in my cousin's room Ma tells me I cannot sleep with them anymore. She does not tell me the reason why, but I imagine Irma does not want me to sleep with her on her small bed. Hearing this makes me kind of angry because Catalina and I slept squished for years when we had to share our bed with Irma and her sister.

•

I now have to sleep with my little nephew Tony. His twin-size bed is in his parents' room's closet. The closet has no doors and it is very small, so there is only room for the bed. I feel bad having to sleep in my brother's room. I am almost twelve and I know he likes having private time with his wife Lola, but there is no room for me anywhere else. Pa, Ma, Gerardo, and Enrique are also staying in Manuel's house. They are sleeping in the second bedroom which is used as a living room during the day. The only two other rooms are the kitchen and the bathroom. With ten people living in this small house, I am lucky I even have a bed to sleep on.

•

It's my first night sleeping with Tony. We are already in bed even though it is only eight o'clock and almost everyone else is still up. The kitchen is only a couple of feet away and I can hear the adults talking and laughing even though the bedroom door is closed. Tony says, I am not sleepy. Can you please tell me a story?

I have never told a story before, but I ask him what he wants the story to be about. He tells me and I cannot believe how easily I come up with an elaborate story about a horse. Lola comes in and puts Galo to bed; he will be sleeping in their bed. A few minutes later she comes in with the baby and puts her in her crib. I keep telling Tony stories, but we have to be very quiet because we do not want to wake up the baby and her crib is only a few feet away. Galo does not seem interested in hearing stories and stays quietly in his parent's bed.

Tomorrow my sister in law, Alicia, will be taking us to school to enroll us. Enrique will be going to elementary school with Carmen and Miguel. Gerardo and I will be going to junior high with Irma. I can hardly wait.

Manuel and Lola come in. It is probably around nine and time to stop telling Tony stories. I really like sleeping with Tony. He is such a calm, sweet kid.

•

Alicia comes to pick up Gerardo and me. She takes us to our soon-to-be school which is only a few blocks away. Once in the office she fills out some forms and I can tell that she is having trouble communicating with the office staff. She finally tells us we are enrolled and can start next week. Gerardo does not seem too happy to hear the good news, but I feel great joy knowing that next week I will be coming to such a big school. The name of it is Sutter Junior High. It has green grass areas all over and a very tall building near the front.

The following Monday, Gerardo and I walk to school with Irma. I have on the outfit Alicia bought me in Tijuana. It is still my best outfit and I am glad to be wearing it again. Irma takes us to the ESL classroom and introduces us to the teacher. He is an older man with silver hair. He is from Cuba and I find out from some people that his English accent is not the best. I do not know how bad his English accent is, but I know his Spanish accent is unlike anything I ever heard before. We have to stay in his classroom most of the day. The only times we will be leaving this classroom is when we go take a math class and when we have P.E. There are only a handful of students in the class and most of them are from Mexico. At lunchtime, Irma comes to pick up Gerardo and me so we can have lunch together. She introduces us to some of her friends before we go to have lunch. Irma used to take ESL classes with them when she first got here. None of them have to take ESL classes anymore, including Irma. Just like her, her friends seem very Americanized and dress nicer than the students in the ESL classroom.

We sit on a grassy area to eat our lunch; we all have ham sandwiches. Most of my classmates are in the cafeteria eating their free lunch. This morning they showed me their lunch ticket. They get one every day because they are on the lunch program. My brother Manuel told Alicia not to enroll us in this program because Teresa came by and told us we cannot be getting free stuff from the government after just arriving in the country. I am glad I am not getting a free lunch. I love ham sandwiches and I enjoy sitting on the grass with Irma and my brother. I am not angry at Irma anymore for not letting me sleep in her bedroom. She is being so kind to us, showing us the school, and introducing us to people. She told us she would be having lunch with us until we get used to the school.

·

I have been in school for a couple months now and I am still eating ham sandwiches for lunch. About a month ago I heard Teresa say to Ma, Why are you still making ham sandwiches for them? Oh, I know, because they are too rich to eat bologna or peanut butter sandwiches. Ma said to her, what can I do? They do not like the taste of bologna or peanut butter. Teresa did not say anything else and left Lola's house. What does she care, I thought, what kind of sandwiches we eat? I know she does not give Ma or Pa any money and we do not spend any time in her house. Manuel and Lola do all the grocery shopping and they never complain about having to buy all the food. Teresa reminds me very much of Josefina, always angry about something. Sometimes she comes by and yells at whoever is in the house for using so much water. When she does this no one says anything to her because we are living in her guest house. Later Manuel says, we pay our share of the water bill and with over ten people in this house taking showers, what does she expect? Maybe if she did not water her vegetable garden so much, the water bill would not be so high. He tells us she is a witch and to just ignore her.

I often wonder how Ma feels about Teresa, but I never ask her. Ma did her best to take good care of her kids when they lived with us in Mexico. She never beat them or even spanked them and she always took Irma to Irapuato to shop. When Teresa sent boxes full of clothes, her kids always got first choice. Now here we are living so close to her and she is always yelling at my brothers and me for one reason or another.

•

I am not eating my ham sandwiches with Irma or my brother anymore. We only ate together for the first two weeks after starting school. Now Irma is back with her friends and Gerardo made some friends. I am eating in the cafeteria with a couple of friends. They get their lunch at the school cafeteria just like almost everyone in the classroom. There are always new students arriving in our class and they start getting free lunch right away. I do not tell Manuel that it seems that every new student arriving gets free lunch because I do not want him asking Alicia to come back to our school to sign us up for the program. I like bringing my lunch in a brown bag just like most of the Americans.

My English gets better every week, but I only get to use it in the classroom. At home we only speak Spanish and that is all I hear as well since we only watch Spanish television. We watch the news and a few Mexican shows. I do not talk much to my cousins in English or Spanish. Carmen and Miguel spend a lot of time playing with their American friends out on the street or at their friends' homes. I know enough English now to realize that they speak English without an accent. They do not have a single Mexican friend, so if I played with them outside I would have to speak English only. But I am embarrassed to do so because I think I have a very heavy accent. Besides they play mostly sports. We never played sports in the Pueblo, so I am sure I am bad at them. Irma does not spend much time outside and she speaks English with an accent. Sometimes I think I could get the nerve to talk to her in English, but she is older than I am and we do not have much in common to talk about.

When I speak English in the classroom I do not feel embarrassed. Everyone has a thick accent including the teacher. We read aloud in class often. This is one of my favorite things to do because I am learning to read faster than most people in the classroom. There are always new students arriving and we have to skip them when we do this activity because they do not know how to read at all.

There are people from all over Mexico in the class and a few from South America. The classroom is over half full now and I am sure it will be completely full by the end of the school year. There is a very pretty girl from Mexico named Maria. She has very light smooth skin, hazel eyes, and smooth, long, light brown hair. All the boys in the class like her, especially since she has a small waist, big breasts, and full hips. I know if she lived back in the Pueblo all the men and boys would be after her as well. They loved girls with shapely figures. Maria always gets A's on her homework papers like I do and I can tell she likes school like I do. But I do not like spending time with her because she always has boys after her and they just ignore me when I am with her. There is also a chubby guy from Nicaragua who is always making jokes and getting into trouble. Gerardo does not cause much trouble in the class, but he never does his homework and does horrible on all the tests.

The math class we have to take is taught by a very kind man whose name is Mr. Sweeney. He has very blue eyes and is tall and thin. He has a teacher's aide that speaks Spanish, but I can tell that he wants to be able to communicate with the students himself. The math class is easy for most of us. We learned this math a couple of years ago in our home countries.

The only other time we have to leave the ESL classroom is when we have to take P.E. I hate P.E. because there are only four ESL students in the class. Most of the American students are either nice to us or simply ignore us, but there are a couple that call three of us wetbacks. They tell us to go to the end of the line when we have to line up for activities. Maria is also in this class, but no one ever picks on her. She is so pretty and sweet. Everyone likes her.

My P.E. locker is next to one of the mean girls, whose name is Connie. She always wears clothes that look brand new and she makes fun of my clothes every chance she gets. She walks completely naked to the showers after P.E. like most of the other girls. She calls me smelly and other names, because I am too embarrassed to take a shower all naked in front of other girls.

There are three Mexican-American girls in the P.E. class. They say they do not speak Spanish and they are mean like the two white girls. They call us wetbacks and I want to tell them their parents were probably wetbacks too. But I keep my mouth shut because I can tell they will beat me up if I say something bad to them.

●

Gerardo, Enrique, and I have been in America about five months. Even though we live in a very crowded house and I get picked on at school, life is much better that it was in Mexico. Ma does not beat any of us and Pa does not beat Ma. We do not have to eat food we do not like or eat all the food on our plates before leaving the table. The fridge always seems to be full with different fruits, vegetables, milk, cheese, and other foods. Manuel buys cookies, chips, and other snacks for us and his kids.

I still like sleeping with Tony. He is in kindergarten and for Valentine's Day he made a heart out of fabric for me. He has told me a few times he is going to marry me when he grows up. I think he is so sweet.

No one ever tells me to do my homework or study for tests. I love school and getting good grades so I always do my homework and prepare for tests. I never see Gerardo or Enrique doing homework since they spend most of their afternoons playing outside. Catalina and Julian go to night school to learn English. Catalina does not seem too interested in school and she misses some nights. Julian always goes and seems eager to get ahead. Pa is still working with Alfonso. Every night he complains about Alfonso, how Alfonso works him so hard even though he is an old man. He also complains about his back every night. He says he needs to go back to Mexico to let his back get better. Everyone ignores him.

Manuel says to him, Pa you are an old man and of course your back is going to hurt doing landscaping work. My back sometimes hurts too, but you have to support your family so you have no choice but to work. I try to make Pa's back feel better by putting hot packs on his back every night.

After weeks of complaining about his back, Pa says he is going back to Mexico and there is nothing anyone can do to stop him. He says, I have been seeing a chiropractor for weeks now and all he does is take X-rays and crack my back. Ma says he is not going back because of his back. He is going back because he does not like to do hard work and it was never his intention to stay here more than a year. Everyone agrees.

After Pa leaves, Gerardo has to start working to help support the family. He is only fourteen, but he lies about his age so he can get Pa's job. I feel bad that he has to quit school, but he does not seem to mind much.

•

A couple of times a month the whole family gets together at a local park for a picnic. I love all the food Lola and Ma prepare, but I hate the baseball games Manuel organizes. We never had balls or bats in Mexico so I do not know how to catch a small ball or hit one with a bat. Manuel and Miguel are usually the team captains and I am always the last one to get picked. I always end up on Miguel's team. Manuel says I am stupid for not knowing how to catch or hit a ball and he does not want me on his team. I wonder how he can be so giving most of the time, but at times so mean and hurtful.

After a few months of sleeping with Tony, Manuel says I cannot sleep with him anymore. I am getting too old and besides Lola is having another baby. Ma, Catalina, Julian, Gerardo, Enrique, and I move in with Alfonso. He is renting a house a few miles away and we can stay there until we find another place. I like living with Alfonso. He never calls my brothers or me stupid

131

like Manuel did and Amelia is very much like Lola. She spends the whole day taking care of her kids, cleaning, and cooking. They now have three sons. The two they brought from Mexico and their first child born in America.

Shortly after Pepe was born, Alfonso got an immigration attorney to help him file for legal status. There is talk that soon people will not be able to file for legal status after they have an American-born child. Alfonso wants to be a legal resident as soon as possible.

Every Friday evening there seems to be a party in Alfonso's backyard. I recognize most of the guys in the backyard, but I do not know their names. These guys, who are only a few years older than me, and Alfonso drink beer and listen to Mexican ranchera music until late in the evening. Since my brothers and I left the Pueblo, many more people have left. Many of them are single guys and Alfonso gets some of them landscaping jobs. Alfonso is a supervisor for a landscaping and sprinkler company. He has the reputation of being a very hard worker and of only recommending guys who work very hard.

We can only stay with Alfonso over the summer. His house is too far away from my junior high and from Enrique's school.

•

Ma, Catalina, my brothers, and I move in with Manuel again. He, Lola and their four kids now live in

132

an apartment a few blocks away from Teresa's house and from my school. Their second daughter, Patricia was born recently. It is only a two-bedroom apartment and Manuel and Lola have to sleep with all their kids again so that Ma, Catalina, and I can have the other bedroom. My three brothers sleep in the living room. Lola never complains about us moving in and she still gets along with Ma.

The apartment building is two stories and our apartment is on the second floor. There are seven apartments upstairs and about the same number below us and on the opposite side. An Asian couple with two kids live next to us; I baby sit their two little kids sometimes. There are a few Americans living in the building and they keep to themselves like everyone else in the building, including the recent Mexican immigrants.

Next to our building, there is an apartment building that looks much newer than ours. It is completely enclosed. All you see from the outside are the beige stucco walls and brown balconies. This building is even quieter than ours and only Americans live there. Lola hardly ever lets her kids play outside because she does not want us to be the noisy tenants.

Lola has her fifth child, another girl, and they cannot keep sharing a room with all their kids including the new baby. So when a one bedroom apartment below is vacated, Ma, Catalina, my brothers, and I move into it. Shortly after finally getting our own place, Catalina tells us she is getting married. She will be marrying a guy from our hometown with whom she has been going out for a few months. Enrique and I could not be happier. Since we got here from Mexico, she has continued to pick on us. Here comes tomato nose, she often says when she sees me entering a room. She calls me other names too and she has many names for Enrique as well. She does not have a stable job or go to school so we all think getting married is the best thing she can do.

Catalina starts planning her wedding and just like I expected, she does not ask me to be part of it. I still do not like her, so I do not mind too much. I am only thirteen years old, but I am much taller than she is. I look like I am fifteen so I could very well be a bridesmaid.

•

It's the mid-seventies. I am in my second year of junior high and Mexican students have continued to arrive. There are now two ESL classrooms and I assume that soon there will be more. Last school year I used to learn every new ESL student's name and I was even able to get to know them a little, but now there are too many coming and I just cannot keep up.

Most of the new students are from different parts of Mexico, but there are some from South America too. Even though I don't get to know the new students, I can tell how shy most of them are when they first get here and how slowly they become more social. I imagine I was the same way when I first arrived. It's not easy coming from poor little towns in Mexico to such a big, plentiful place.

There is a girl from Tijuana who arrived last year who still acts shy. Her name is Patricia. She has blemish-free creamy white skin, short wavy black hair, a pointy nose and dark eyes with curly eyelashes. I think she is prettier than Maria. I talk to her sometimes and I can tell she does not care about how pretty she is. I would like to be friends with her, but she never has much to say and I think she just does not like people. I wonder what her life was like in Mexico that made her act this way, but I never have the nerve to ask her.

A girl from Guadalajara just arrived. She is from a small rancho and she acts very shy. I think it will not be long before she changes because she looks American. She has long blond hair, blue eyes, and tanned skin.

The white girl named Connie continues to pick on me and the Mexican-American girls are mean to me too. They call me wetback and ask me if I buy my clothes at garage sales. There is one Mexican-American girl that is really mean. She is short and chunky and has bad skin. Every time she insults me I think about all the names I could call her, but I never say anything to her. She looks like she does not care about school or getting into trouble and would beat me up in no time if I said anything to her. I am not afraid of getting beaten up, but I love school and learning and I would die if I ever got suspended.

•

The day of Catalina's wedding finally arrives. Ma bought me a navy blue pantsuit to wear today. I do not really like it, but I do not say anything. I wear mostly hand-me-downs, so I am happy that I have a new outfit even if the long sleeves are a little too short.

At the wedding I sit way in the back and cannot really see what is going on. I cannot wait until it is over so we can go to the reception. Catalina often talked about her wedding reception. We got the biggest hall we could find, she would say, and we are inviting tons of people from the Pueblo.

When the ceremony is finally over, we head to the reception with my cousin Juan. Juan has only been in America a little over a year, but he already has a car and a driver's license. His car is pretty old, but he keeps it very clean. Ma sits in the front and Enrique, Gerardo, and I sit in the back.

Shortly after leaving the church and as Juan is making a left turn, we feel the impact of another car. Like everyone else in the car I am not wearing a seatbelt. I smash into Enrique and then against the side of the car. The car ends up a few feet away from the intersection and Juan is able to drive it to a gas station just a few feet away. He gets out of the car and finds out that the driver of the other car admits she tried to run a red light. A short time later we are taken to the hospital to be checked out. We all have X-rays taken and are told we are all fine and can go home.

By the time my brother Jose comes to pick us up, it is already nighttime. I can take you to the reception if you still feel like going, he says to us. We tell him we do, but when we get there, the music is so loud it makes my bad headache even worse. Ma does not feel good either. We ask Jose to takes us home.

Many months later Ma gets a few thousand dollars as compensation for the accident. She says she is going to use all of it to build a new kitchen and a bathroom in our house in Mexico. Enrique, Gerardo, and I get nothing.

•

It's my last year in junior high. I am now in ninth grade and I am not taking ESL classes anymore. Our teacher felt that Maria, a couple of other students, and I were proficient enough in English to take regular classes. Most of the students who arrived at around the same time as me are still in the ESL classroom and I was surprised when the teacher told me I would be taking regular classes. Maria told me at the time that I should not be surprised because I always do well on tests.

I like being in the regular classes because I am learning so much more than in the ESL classroom. One of my favorite classes is U.S. history. Learning about this country makes me love it even more.

I am doing well in regular classes even though I do not really participate in class. I think I have a thick accent and I feel embarrassed talking. I am able to pronounce most words, but I find the words starting with "w" very difficult to pronounce. We do not have the sound for "w" in Spanish and I find the word "world" particularly hard. Still I practice this word every day.

•

I hurt my ankle at school playing basketball in P.E. My brothers and I have never been to a doctor since we got here and Ma does not know what to do. When my foot started swelling up, I had the feeling Ma would not take me to a doctor even though my foot looked really bad. For three years I have failed the vision and hearing tests given at school annually. When I give Ma the note and tell her what it means, she just puts it in a drawer and does not say anything.

It is very painful moving my foot and walking on it. The side of it looks odd with a bump on it the size of an orange. Manuel comes over to look at it and says that is what I get for being so stupid. Late in the evening Alfonso comes to look at it. He says it looks very bad and he should probably take me to the hospital. Ma tells him Alicia is coming to look at it later on and she will know whether it is fractured or not. Alicia comes over and says it's just a sprain. She massages it and says she will be back every night this week to massage it. The swelling goes down, but I cannot walk on my foot so I am unable to go to school the rest of the week.

•

The apartment manager kicks us out of our apartment. I imagine it's because there are so many of us living in a one bedroom apartment. Julian says it's because she wants all the Mexicans out of the building.

Luckily Manuel finds a two-story, four-bedroom apartment with a big living room, dining room, and kitchen to which we can all move in together. A month later we move into the new apartment.

We are all happy with the size of the apartment. The four bedrooms and one bathroom are on the second floor. The living room, dining room, kitchen, and another bathroom are on the first. The living room has shaggy green carpet and it is big just like Manuel said. Julian, Gerardo, and Enrique don't have to sleep in it since they finally have a bedroom. I share one of the other rooms with Ma.

Our satisfaction with the apartment does not last long. Ma and Lola cannot believe Manuel did not notice how bad this neighborhood really is. Most of the people living here are recent Mexican immigrants and they call this block of apartments, Tijuanita (Little TJ).

Every evening many of the men drink beer outside and play loud Mexican ranchera music in the parking lot. On weekends they stay out until late at night playing their music and drinking beer. Ma says they must be peeing on the back wall near the trash bins because when she takes the trash out she always smells pee. My nieces and nephews are never allowed to play outside and I never go out either. Ma and Lola always sweep the outside of the apartment, but it does not seem to help. There is a liquor store across the street and people are always walking there to buy snacks. They eat them on their way back and drop their trash on the ground once they are done with them. Sometimes Ma tells me to sweep outside and I feel like sweeping the whole block, but what good would it do? It would probably be dirty again the next day.

When I come home from school, I always see guys standing in front of the liquor store and I often see women standing in front of their apartments. Ma cannot stand these women. She calls them lazy and says, why don't these women get a broom and sweep in front of their apartments instead of just standing by their front door?

Before I get to our block I pass clean, quiet streets. These streets have houses with green, well kept lawns. Americans live there and I feel sorry for the ones that live close to our block.

Sometimes on weekends Catalina comes to visit. She comes up to my room and calls me "encuartada" (someone who never leaves their room). I do not really care what she calls me. I love staying in my room reading. Back in Mexico we did not have any books other than the math, grammar, and history books required for school. Gerardo was somehow able to buy comic books, but I did not like comic books so I never read. I now read every chance I get. I read all kinds of paperbacks. I liked reading *One Flew Over the Cuckoo's Nest* so much that I read it twice.

•

Shortly after I graduate from junior high, we move into the apartment building in Canoga Park where my brother Jose lives. Manuel moves into a two-bedroom apartment and Ma, my brothers, and I get a one-bedroom since that is all we can afford. Some of the people living here are recent immigrants. Like us, they are quiet and keep to themselves. Sometimes on Friday evenings, Jose and a couple of other guys drink beer out in the parking lot, but they do not play any music, nor of course, pee on the walls. They stay out for a short while and then go into their apartments like everyone else in the building.

•

It's the late 70's and I am attending Cleveland High School. I should actually be attending Canoga Park High because that is where I live now, but I heard that Cleveland High is a better school. If we had stayed at the apartments called Tijuanita, Cleveland High would be much closer. But I am still glad we moved because we now live in a clean quiet neighborhood.

I am fourteen years old, in tenth grade, and I like high school much more than junior high. There are only a handful of immigrant students in the school and we all sit together at lunchtime. No one ever picks on us. It seems that in high school most people are too worried about their appearance and trying to be popular to take the time to pick on us.

●

My brother Jose got me a weekend job cleaning the offices of the landscaping and sprinkler company he works for. Every Saturday morning I go with him to his job and while I am cleaning the offices, he usually does maintenance on the work trucks and equipment. All I have to do is dust, vacuum, take the garbage out, and clean the small kitchen and the bathroom sinks. Jose tells me I am too young to be cleaning toilets so he cleans them for me. He tells me maybe someday I can work as a receptionist or even a secretary here. I want to tell him, we are in America and I can be a lot more than that, but I just smile at him and nod my head.

I quit the office cleaning job and look for a job at a fast food restaurant. Most of the people working at these restaurants are white students around my age and I think it would be fun working with them. I am now fifteen years old.

●

Pa calls and says he wants Ma, my brothers, and I to go back to Mexico. He says his back has healed and the government finally gave them the farm land that he and some other men had been fighting many years for.

When I get on the phone with him, I tell him I do not want to go back to Mexico. I tell him that I am going to school here and I like it here very much. He says, you are still a minor and I can get a visa, come get you, and bring you back even if I have to tie you down. I start crying. He tells me he promises he will pay for me to go to high school in Mexico, but I do not believe him.

I get off the phone and tell Ma I am not going back to Mexico even if he comes and drags me by my feet.

Julian, Gerardo, and Enrique don't mind going back. Julian has been working full-time, while going to night school for years; he is getting tired of such a stressful life. Gerardo has been working full-time for a few years now without a vacation. Enrique is in school, but he never does his homework and gets horrible grades. Ma thinks Gerardo and Enrique are doing drugs and it would be better for them to be back in the Pueblo.

A month or so later, Ma and my brothers go back to Mexico. I go live with Jose and his wife in the apartment below. Living with Jose does not work out. Jose likes staying up until late at night watching television. The TV is the living room where I sleep and I cannot sleep even if he has it on very low.

I ask Manuel if I can live with him. He says yes even though his two-bedroom apartment is already crowded with him, Lola, their five kids, and Lola's sister who moved in with them a couple of months back.

•

I am still fifteen years old and I am now attending Canoga Park High School. I finally got my first real job. I am working at a Der Wienerschnitzel. I wanted to get a job at a different fast food restaurant because I never saw any young people working at this one. But I had to get a job as soon as possible after Ma left because I cannot be asking Manuel for money.

I am glad to be working for many reasons, including having to speak English. At school all my friends are Mexican and we only speak Spanish. When I am in the classroom, I am too embarrassed to speak because I think my accent is too heavy. At home I only speak Spanish.

At this job I am forced to speak English. There is a Mexican-American girl working here who also goes to Canoga Park High, but her Spanish is much worse than my English so we only speak English. There is an older Mexican-American lady also working here, but her Spanish is also very bad. The other people working here are white and they do not speak any Spanish. I am glad to finally be able to practice the English I have been learning for years.

I stay at this job for less than a year and then get a job as a cashier at a drug store nearby. The name of the drug store is Clark Drugs. It's a big drug store. It has six regular registers, a pharmacy, and four separate departments: liquor, photo, cosmetics, and an ice cream

144

department. I will be able to join their union even though I will just be a part time employee.

●

Manuel buys a three bedroom house in Reseda. Reseda is in the San Fernando Valley like Canoga Park, but seems far away from my high school. Still, I decide to stay at Canoga Park High. I am tired of switching schools and besides my job at the drug store is near the school.

My high school graduation is approaching and no one seems to care even though I will be the first person in my family to be getting a high school diploma. I know my brothers and my sisters-in-law are busy working and raising their kids, but no one has even said congratulations to me.

At work most of the people working part-time are high school students. The ones that are graduating are very excited. Nancy, a pretty girl with wavy red hair, says she cannot wait to graduate and go off to college. She goes to Canoga Park High also and did very well in advanced placement courses so she was able to get into the college of her choice. Wayne, an Asian guy who always got good grades will be going off to college as well.

My Mexican friends and I are not excited about our graduation. We never talk about college or what we will do once we graduate. One of my better friends, named Silvia, just got to the United States two years ago and does not speak very good English. I hope she can get a decent job once we graduate.

I still love school and learning and I actually feel sad that I am almost finished with school. I always felt that college was out of my reach, so I never looked into the requirements for getting into one.

The day of my graduation comes and I invite Alicia to the ceremony. She was the one who enrolled my brothers and me in school when we first got here and I always signed her name on school documents that needed the signature of our guardian. My brothers and sisters do not like her. They say she loves to gossip about everyone in the family and that she takes advantage of our nice brother Jose. I do not know what they are talking about. She has always seemed like a kind person to me.

•

It has been a few weeks since I graduated from high school and I am working almost full time at Clark Drugs making decent money. The manager gave me mostly day shifts because I am working so many more hours. My life is pretty easy now, but I am not happy. I miss school and I feel there is so much more I need to learn. I decide to enroll at the local community college. Maybe later I can even transfer to a four-year college. After all, I am in America, where anything is possible.

•

Every weekday now I take the bus to Pierce Community College and I am thankful that the school is conveniently located. All I have to do each morning is walk a few yards to the bus stop on Victory Boulevard, wait a while, and get on a bus that drops me off in front of the school. After school is over, I take the same bus back to Manuel's house. I do homework, get something to eat, and take another bus to work. The drugstore closes at ten o'clock, but after it closes we have to count money and clean up so we are not finished until eleven. By the time I get off, my brother Jose is waiting for me to take me home. This is my routine on most days and I love my life. When I do have some free time, I take my nephew Tony out someplace or stay home and play with him and his siblings. I never watch TV or go out on dates, but I do not mind. I am going to school and that is the only thing that matters.

Ma, Gerardo, and Enrique come to visit from Mexico. I normally share a room with my niece Patty, but after Ma arrives she has to go sleep with her two sisters and let Ma use her bed.

Ma asks me how I was able to get such a good job working as a cashier at Clark Drugs. I tell her I just applied and got the job right away. When we lived in Canoga Park, she used to shop at Clark Drugs all the time. Compared to the stores in Mexico, this store seemed gigantic to her. I know that in her eyes being a cashier is a very good position, so I do not tell her it's just a part-time job to get me through school. And I do not tell her I started as a cashier, but that I now work in the cosmetics department, which is better than just being a cashier.

Ma and Gerardo go back to Mexico after a couple of months, but Enrique stays with Manuel. I imagine he did not like going to school in Mexico.

•

Even though I do not think my job at the drugstore is a very good job, I really enjoy working here. Most of the people I work with are white and they are hard working and respectful. I have been here for more than two years and I am still the only young immigrant working here. The only other immigrant is an older man whose name is Fernando. He seems to be in his late thirties or early forties and when I met him I could tell he was from Guadalajara. He has green eyes, light brown wavy hair, and light skin. He looks Spanish and I have met many people from Guadalajara that look like him. He works in the photo department and always wears collar shirts and a tie. I hardly ever have a chance to talk to him since he only works the dayshift, but I can tell he has been in this country for many years even though he still has a thick accent.

A lady named Sue also works in the photo department. She is very tall and has blue eyes and short blond hair. She seems to be in her late twenties or early thirties and jokes around with everyone she works with. She seems very smart when I talk to her in the lunch room and I wonder if she is happy having this job as her full-time job.

The liquor department is at the front of the store and the chips and other snacks are located there too. So every time I have a break I go there to buy a snack. The guy who usually works the liquor department is also white and seems smart as well.

The cosmetics department is in the back of the store near the pharmacy and two middle-aged white ladies work the day shift. They are both married and have kids. One of them drives here from Valencia, which is quite far, and once told me that it is worth driving the far distance because here we have a union, automatic raises, and medical insurance. I do not get the medical insurance because I am only a part time employee, but I do get the automatic raises after I work a certain number of hours.

I like working in the cosmetics department much more than being a cashier. The managers do not bother me and I like taking care of customers and stocking shelves. The gift-wrap department is by the back entrance, right next to the ice cream and candy department. If you work the cosmetic counter, you are also responsible for gift wrapping. No one likes working the ice cream department and whoever is assigned to it takes off to do something else as soon as the customers are helped. Therefore when I am there to gift-wrap, I end up having to serve a few ice cream cones to customers. I just cannot tell them they have to wait for the person assigned to that department.

The checkout registers are at the center of the store and the manager's booth is right next to them. Two or three of the checkouts are always open and the managers call for other cashiers when they are needed. Two of the backup cashiers are young, pretty moms, who roll their eyes when they have to stop stocking the shelves to check out customers. There are two other ladies who also stock shelves during the day. One of them is in her fifties and the other one in her sixties. The assistant managers never joke around with them like they do with the young moms.

The head manager is an older man who seems to be in his late forties or early fifties. Most employees are afraid of him because he looses his temper easily. I think he is a kind man who just wants you to do your job right.

All the daytime employees have been here since I started and I enjoyed working with them in the summer when I was working the dayshift. But now I only see them for a few minutes during the week since their shift ends at six o'clock and that is when mine starts.

Most of the night employees are high school and college students and they do not stay long. There are two part-time employees who have been here since I started. Both of them are Japanese-American, one is named Wayne and the other is named Todd.

Todd is the best-looking Asian guy I have ever seen. He looks like a Japanese movie star. He is tall and athletic and I have had I crush on him since I started working here. I love the way he smiles when he talks and how kind he seems to be. When I started working here I used to get so nervous when I saw him in the break room that I could not eat the snack I had just bought or even say more than just a few words to him. I feel more comfortable around him now, but I still feel warm all over and a little nervous when I am near him.

Todd just graduated from college and is now looking for a full time job. I will miss him very much when he is gone, but I have always felt he was way too good for me so I need to forget about him. I know he dated a couple of girls working here. One of them still works here; her name is Michelle and she is beautiful. She is in her early twenties, has long blond hair, blue eyes, and a perfect figure. The ladies I work with in the cosmetics department tell me I have a cute figure and I know the guys working here think I am attractive. I do not feel like an illegal alien anymore, but I am a girl who grew up dirt poor and I cannot see someone like me going out with Todd.

It is the early eighties and I am surprised I am still the only young immigrant working at the drug store since so many Mexicans and immigrants from South America have settled in this neighborhood since I started working here. Most of them do not speak any English and I have to translate for them when they need help in the pharmacy. Sometimes when I am telling the pharmacist what the person needs he gets impatient when he realizes this person should really be seeing a doctor. I do not like to tell people that the pharmacist cannot help them and that they have to see a doctor because I can tell by the way they look at me that they cannot afford to go see one.

One of the assistant managers says this neighborhood is going downhill and that he is moving with his wife and kids up to Washington State as soon as he is able to. When I hear him say this, I pray to God that this neighborhood never looks like the neighborhood called Little TJ where I lived not long ago.

•

Pierce College is located in Woodland Hills and so far I am the only immigrant here from Canoga Park High School. I wonder what the immigrant students I went to school with are doing with their lives and I wish some of them came here. Most of the students at Pierce are white, but lately I have been seeing many students from Iran. There are a few Latinos and I have become very good friends with one from South America. Her name is Sofia and she is actually my neighbor. She is renting a guest room in a house just a couple of doors away from Manuel's house. We met at the bus stop when school started and we were happy when we checked our class schedules and realized we had algebra together.

It's been some time since we started the algebra class and Sofia is having a hard time in the class. She keeps getting C's and D's on the tests and I try to help her since I get all A's. Sometimes she gets very discouraged and says she might stop coming to school after this year.

•

I have the afternoon off and I go see Sofia. She knew I was coming, but when I get to her place she is on her bed crying, her mascara is running and her long wavy black hair is messy and on her face. She says, my boyfriend was here and he gave me a hard time because I did not shave my underarms. He also told me I need to lose a few pounds because he does not like going to bed with a chunky girl. You are not chunky, I tell her. But she tells me she has gained a few extra pounds since she started dating her boyfriend. I am always trying to lose weight, but I just can't, she says.

Sofia is a pretty girl and I cannot believe her boyfriend could be so cruel to her. Why are you going out with someone so mean? I say to her. She tells me she loves him even though it is not the first time he has given her a hard time.

I met her boyfriend at school a few weeks ago. He is from Iran and he is kind of short, a little overweight, and with plenty of body hair on his arms. How can this hairy, overweight guy give my friend a hard time? I tell Sofia she needs to dump him and find someone who appreciates how pretty and kind she is.

A few weeks later an Iranian guy I met at school asks me out. He seems kind and treats me well so I decide to go out with him. We go out in his van a few times after school. But when we go to his house to do homework he tells me he gives answers to tests to other Iranian students. Then in the afternoon he tries to take my clothes off and I realize I want nothing to do with him. I later go out with a guy from Korea. We do not seem to have too much in common and we stop going out after a few afternoon dates.

•

Manuel buys a new car and lets me have his old one. So I no longer have to take the bus and my brother Jose does not need to give me a ride home after my night shift at the drugstore. He always told me it was not hard for him to give me a ride home since he lives so close to my work, but I felt bad anyway because my shift does not end until close to eleven on most nights and Manuel's house is a few miles away.

I take the driving test and have no trouble passing it since I took driver's education at school.

•

It is now my second year at the two-year community college, but it will not be my last year in school. Over the summer I felt so sad thinking that in a year I would have my AA degree and be finished with school, that I went to Cal State Northridge to get a book that would tell me what grade point average I needed to have, and which courses I needed to take to transfer there.

I got very good grades my first year at Pierce College so my grade point average is well above the 3.3 requirement for transfer students and I have already taken many of the courses required to transfer. I feel confident I will get accepted once I apply, even though I have never talked to a counselor about what else I should be doing to get accepted.

I do not recall ever seeing a counselor in junior high. I never saw one in high school and I do not see the need to start seeing one now. In high school you were given a list indicating which classes were required to graduate and how many credits you needed to have. When I first enrolled at Pierce, I got a booklet that indicated what general education classes and what classes related to my major I needed to take to get my AA degree. Now I have the book for Cal State Northridge that gives me all the information I need to transfer there.

In high school I liked all the classes I was taking, so when I enrolled at Pierce it was difficult deciding on a major. I eventually decided on accounting because I felt it would not be hard to get an accounting job after graduation.

●

My second year at Pierce is even more fun than the first. I love all my classes and I have more friends. I am very good friends with a girl from Mexico that just started school here. Her name is Veronica and she just graduated from Canoga Park High School.

When I was in high school I saw her in the cafeteria all the time, sitting at the table where all the Mexicans sat, but we never really talked. She has a heavy accent even though she has been in this country for a long time. I do not know if she is an illegal immigrant since we never talk about our immigration status.

My other best friend is Chinese. She changed her Chinese name to Emily. She has only been here for a couple of years, but she already speaks very good English. I have been to her house and met her mom and her two sisters. Her dad is a pilot and is gone most of the time so when I come over they always invite me to stay for dinner. Their homemade Chinese food is great, but what is even better is taking part in their dinner conversation. They talk about school so much, how they did on their recent tests, which classes they like the most, and what they have to do to get A's in their classes. I have never in my life had a conversation like this in my family and know I never will. I have told Emily how I think it's great that her family cares so much about education, but she said she gets tired of being expected to get A's in every subject. Her sisters get straight A's and when Emily brings home a B her mom is not too happy.

•

Todd comes to visit us at work. It has been quite a few months since he quit after getting a full time job as a sales representative. I can hear him talking to the assistant manager and I know it will not be long before he comes over to talk to me since we became friends before he quit. I started feeling butterflies in my stomach the minute I heard his voice and now I am so excited about seeing him I am unable to finish the nail polish price change I am supposed to be working on.

By the time he comes over to talk to me I have managed to calm myself down and I tell him I am planning on transferring to his former school, Cal State Northridge. He tells me he is very happy for me and that he is sure I will do well. He says he really likes his new job, but sometimes kind of misses this place. I want to tell him how much I miss him, but cannot get the words to come out. He looks at me in a way he never looked at me before. His voice gets softer and he says to me, would you like to go out sometime?

I look at him with disbelief. I cannot believe the guy I have had a crush on for years has just asked me out. He gives me a nervous look and I realize that I have been in shock for a few seconds and have not responded to him. Of course I'll go out with you, I finally say. We make plans to go to the movies before he leaves the store.

•

It is the third time I go out with Todd, but the first time Manuel is home when Todd comes to pick me up. Manuel is not happy to hear I will be going out with a guy. I want to tell him I am already nineteen years old and that it is only the third time I'm going out on a nighttime date. But I do not say anything to him and run out of the house.

The next day Lola tells me Manuel does not want me to keep living with them if I am going to be dating guys. She also says they might be losing their house because they have been unable to pay the mortgage over the last few months. Maybe it's a good time for you to find another place to live, she says to me sadly. I cannot imagine not going out with Todd so I ask my cousin Carmen if I can move in with them. She says her mom is in Mexico right now, but she is sure it will be okay with her.

●

Teresa is surprised to find me in her house when she comes back from Mexico. I tell her what happened with Manuel and she says I can stay as long as I pay her rent, give her money for food and utilities, and do chores.

I know Teresa is much different than Lola and Manuel and will not try to make my life easier just because I am putting myself through school. Manuel would never let me pay him money for rent or give him money for food or utilities. After I told him I did not think it was right for me not to pay for anything he said, okay you can buy clothes for the girls. As for Lola, she never let me do any chores. Whenever she saw me washing dishes or doing other chores, she would say, don't you have homework to do?

•

It has been a couple of months since I started going out with Todd. He even took me to meet his parents. They live in a quiet residential street in Northridge, a couple of blocks away from "Tijuanita." I wonder how they feel about living close to such a bad neighborhood. I do not think I will ever be able to tell Todd I used to live a couple of blocks away. He would ask me where and I would have to tell him.

•

Spring break is coming up and Carmen and I decide to go visit our hometown in Mexico. It will be our first time going back since we first arrived in America. Carmen is working full-time and says she needs a vacation. I need to get away from Todd. Since I started seeing him, my test grades have dropped because I am always thinking about him and I don't spend as much time doing homework or studying. I love him more than anyone in the world, but school is still more important to me. I do not want to risk lowering my grade point average and not being able to transfer to Cal State Northridge.

I tell Todd I will be going back to Mexico and do not know exactly when I will be coming back. It is painful telling him this, but I keep telling myself that once I am finished with school I can probably get back with him.

•

We arrive in our hometown late in the evening and have to wait until the morning to see how much the Pueblo has changed since we left. It is the early eighties and we know many people have left the Pueblo, but we do not really know what to expect.

The house I grew up in looks exactly the same on the outside, but once inside I see the new kitchen, bathroom, and bedroom that were built with the money Ma got from the car accident and also the money I sent her. The new rooms do not look very good to Carmen and me. All the rooms have brick walls, but the walls are covered with gray cement and look unfinished. The floors also look unfinished. They are made of gray, rough cement. When I see the bathroom, I do not look forward to taking a shower the next day. It is about half the size of a regular bedroom and it feels cold. The only things in it are a shower head, a small sink, and a toilet. I check the bathroom door to see if it works well. I would hate for someone to come in when I am taking a shower for the shower has no doors or curtains. Ma seems to be happy with the house and we tell her it looks good.

We wake up the next day to a typical warm sunny day. Ma has a small refrigerator now, but still has to go to the plaza first thing in the morning because the refrigerator is practically empty. She comes back with fresh bread and the meat she will be using to make Pa and Julian breakfast. Carmen and I get up. Carmen eats some of the sweet Mexican bread right away. My favorite Mexican bread is a starchy roll with a thick crust. I do not see any in the bread basket and I ask Ma about it. She tells me they only make it in the afternoon and I cannot wait to have some. Other than my Tia Victoria's whole wheat gorditas (biscuits), it's the only thing from Mexico I miss. I am sure I will be eating it every day until we leave.

Pa and Julian come home around ten to have breakfast. Early this morning I heard them both in the kitchen getting ready to go work at the farm. Pa, who looks about the same as the last time I saw him, says to me, you need to drink a lot of the milk we just brought from the farm. You are so skinny, if it wasn't for your chunky cheeks you would look like a skeleton.

I do not love my father as much as I did when I was a kid and do not really care if he thinks I look almost like a skeleton. In America, people I work with think I have a cute figure and the manager tells me I am looking prettier all the time. It won't be long before I go back and I am already starting to miss my new country.

After breakfast Carmen and I walk to Josefina's house to visit our cousins. We are shocked to see how quiet the Pueblo has become. People have continued to leave the Pueblo for El Norte since the time we left and now it seems that more than half of the population is gone. We do not see kids playing on the street anymore or women standing in front of their homes gossiping with their neighbors. When we walk past the plaza, we see hardly any men there. It feels like the life has been sucked out of the pueblo and we know we will be bored here.

●

When I come back from Mexico, I do not call Todd to tell him that I am back. I want to see him, but I know I need to stay away from him.

A couple of months after I come back Todd comes to visit us at the drugstore and is surprised to see me there. I thought you were still in Mexico, he says. I have been back for a while, I tell him. You didn't really think I would be gone for a long time, did you? I was only gone during spring break. You know I cannot miss school if I want to transfer.

Todd's eyes no longer look surprised, they now look sad. He tells me he is already dating someone else. I tell him it is fine; I do not have time to be dating right now anyway. I feel so much pain inside, but I know it's for the best. He is twenty-four years old and he is probably dating someone closer to his age. I know in my heart that once I am done with school, I will be with him again.

●

Living with Teresa gets more intolerable by the day and I try to spend as little time as possible in her house. She and Carmen fight all the time. Every time they fight, they call each other names, go into their separate bedrooms, and slam their doors. Miguel who lives here too leaves the house as soon as he hears them start to argue.

I never know what they fight about since I step outside when they start yelling and I try to ignore them. But I think Teresa is probably at fault. She seems angry all the time, and she gives me a hard time too. She tells me she does not care if I am busy all the time with school and work. I still have to clean the bathroom every week and I had better start doing a better job at it. When she goes to the grocery store and I happen to be home, she yells at me and tells me that I had better help her put the groceries away even though I hardly ever eat at home.

The other day she even told me she thinks I am wasting my time going to college. I do not know why you are going to school, she said. You do not have what it takes to make it. What kind of person tells a young person that they are wasting their time going to school? I thought at the time.

A few months later I transfer to Cal State Northridge. After my sister Catalina hears I am having a very hard time living with Teresa, she tells me that she and her husband will be renting a house in the valley soon and I can move in with them.

Living with Catalina is much easier than living with Teresa. Catalina is not mean like she used to be. She does not want me to help out around the house so I can concentrate on my school work. When she goes grocery shopping, I give her money and she buys me my favorite foods.

I have been at Cal State Northridge for over a year now and I still love school, but I am starting to get tired.

For a few years now I have been spending most of my time going to school and working. I almost never get enough sleep and I hardly ever have time to date. The only time I have fun is when I take Catalina's kids out. She has two boys and a girl. Catalina spends most of the day cleaning the house, doing laundry, and cooking. She hardly ever takes her kids out so when I have time I take them to the movies and to the playground.

At school I have made some new friends. When I started school here, I saw two immigrant girls I used to be friends with back in junior high. They told me they were accounting majors like me, but they were having a tough time in their classes and I think they dropped out. I was not friends with them in high school, but I was glad to see other Mexican immigrants here. I thought I would be friends with them again. Now, with them gone, I feel like I am the only Mexican immigrant here. I belong to the Latino business club and I think every Latino in it was born here. My two best friends are both Mexican-American and they both belong to this club, but unlike the other members they do not put me down because I am a Mexican immigrant with an accent.

●

Ma and Gerardo come back from Mexico. Gerardo got stabbed in the Pueblo and Ma, fearing he might get stabbed again, wasted no time asking my brothers for help crossing the border. They are now living with Catalina too. But I know it won't be long before I have to look for an apartment for Ma, Gerardo, and me since Ma and Catalina are not getting along. Enrique is living with Alfonso now and he will probably move in with us when we get our own place.

•

A couple of months later, we move into a one bedroom apartment. I now have a bookkeeping job so I have weekends and afternoons off.

It is Saturday evening and I am trying to do school work in the bedroom. Gerardo and Enrique are in the living room playing loud music and probably doing drugs. Ma is at either Alfonso's or Manuel's house like the last two weekends. I know my brothers will not listen to me and turn their Led Zeppelin music down, but I come out to ask them anyway. Gerardo is on the couch. His head is down and his long hair covers half his face. He is trying to stick a needle in his arm. He looks up when he hears me coming. His eyes are red and he looks like he is going to pass out. He asks me if I can inject the needle in his arm. I say, no way. Enrique is passed out on the floor, but I am not too worried about him. I heard that he does not do the really bad drugs like Gerardo. I go back in the bedroom and put my school work away. I had heard that my brothers did drugs, but I had no idea it was this bad.

•

My graduation is approaching and I am scared. I will be getting a degree in accounting, but I do not feel I am ready to be a professional. I have had a couple of bookkeeping jobs and I do not find accounting difficult. But how can I be an accountant when almost all of the people I know are gardeners, maids, or factory workers? I did better in accounting classes than some of the people interviewing with the Big Eight accounting firms, but I do not feel I am ready to have a good job. I always felt that in America anything is possible if you work hard enough. But now that I am about to graduate, I feel I need time to realize that my dream of having a college degree will actually come true.

•

I am at Cal State Northridge wearing a cap and gown and all I am thinking about is how much I love America. I am the first person in my family to graduate from college and I know this would not be possible if I was not in this country. Ma, Lola, Catalina, and Catalina's husband, Jose, are here, and I can tell that they are proud of me. Catalina's kids are also here, but they are too little to understand what is going on.

I have not interviewed with any accounting firms, but I know I will do it when I feel ready. I have decided to apply with a temp agency and work at different accounting jobs for a while. I have been going to school and working since I was fifteen and I feel drained and exhausted.

I do not feel as scared now. I know America is a great country with countless opportunities and I feel blessed to be here. When I was a kid in Mexico, I did not once look forward to my future. But ever since that sunny Monday morning when I woke up on my cousin's bed, at the age of eleven, I have looked forward to my future every single day. I know I will be able to get a good job when I am ready. And as I wait to get my diploma, I say to myself, Thank God for America.

Epilogue

It has been many years since I graduated from college and I did accomplish my American dream of having a career. By the time I was in my mid-twenties I was already working for a mid-size local CPA firm preparing tax returns for millionaire clients and for corporations.

I feel extreme love and gratitude towards this Great Country and I have tried to be a good citizen by contributing as much as possible. I have been a Sierra Club leader, a soccer coach, a Girl Scout leader, and a Girls Group leader.

I married a wonderful man and we have three great children. I have also tried to pay back this country by raising kids that do respect Mexico, but that love and have loyalty to only one country, America.

Final Thoughts

I became a legal resident thanks to the Amnesty Act of 1986. Even though I felt extremely thankful and happy to be a legal resident on paper, by the time the law passed I felt so much love and loyalty for America that in my heart I was already a citizen (I became a naturalized citizen in 1996). I also felt that this great country would not deport someone who was brought here as a child and on whom thousands of dollars had already been spent to educate.

Right after the law passed, I filled out the paperwork and put together the documents needed to qualify for amnesty for myself and for many of my relatives. This period was a hectic and crazy time, and I heard stories about people trying desperately to buy fake documents in order to quality.

I do not know if another amnesty will eventually pass (to us, being able to remain in this country legally is amnesty, even if fees have to be paid), but comments I hear such as "We do not have to assimilate because there will be more people like us coming" and "This land used to be ours and we are just taking it back" worry me immensely.

When I hear these comments I want to say to people, where is your appreciation for everything this country has done for us? Where would we be if it was not for this country? But I do not because I actually like these people. I just do not understand how they can possibly feel the way that they do after all America has done for us.

Also, when I hear Mexican activists say on television that it's the United States and its trade policies that are at fault for so many people coming here illegally. I wish I could say to these people that there was no NAFTA in the 1960's and 1970's when my brothers and sister came here because of lack of jobs and opportunities. Maybe NAFTA did hurt some people and forced them to come here to be able to feed their families, but this is a very small portion.

If anyone is to blame, it is the elite class and the politicians of Mexico. The rich people in Mexico would have been happy to keep us as poor ignorant peasants. They never wanted to invest in their towns and provide opportunities for the poor. And the government was – and still is – too corrupt and inefficient to help us.

For years I felt disturbed every time I heard President Vicente Fox refer to Mexicans coming to America as a "migration phenomenon". People fleeing their home country because if they stay they face a lifetime of poverty and deprivation is not a "migration phenomenon". It is a desperate journey of hope.

Vicente Fox and the current president of Mexico have criticized the United States many times saying the U.S. is making a grave mistake not giving amnesty to millions of Mexicans. How can these two presidents criticize the United States? When they themselves – as well as most Mexican presidents – have neglected poor Mexican people for a great number of years?

For decades America has been giving millions of Mexicans the hope that the Mexican government has brazenly failed to give to its poor citizens. But America cannot continue to do so, for its culture may be at stake.

Now more than ever, the Mexican government and the elite class of Mexico need to provide opportunities for poor Mexican citizens. And not expect another nation to provide jobs and opportunity for the poor people they have neglected for hundreds of years.

CPSIA information can be obtained at www.ICGtesting.com
Printed in the USA
LVOW06s1228180813

348392LV00002B/674/P